# Children
## of the
# Yellow Kid

ROBERT C. HARVEY

# Children of the Yellow Kid

## The Evolution of the American Comic Strip

WITH CONTRIBUTIONS BY

BRIAN WALKER

RICHARD V. WEST

FRYE ART MUSEUM, SEATTLE

1998

IN ASSOCIATION WITH THE UNIVERSITY OF WASHINGTON PRESS, SEATTLE AND LONDON

*Front cover and frontispiece:* **1.** Richard Felton Outcault (1863-1928), **McFadden's Row of Flats** (October 18, 1896 - January 23, 1898). October 25, 1896. Color proof-sheet, 19 × 14 1/2 in. (483 × 368 mm). Richard D. Olsen Collection, The Ohio State University Cartoon Research Library.

When Hearst lured Outcault away in October 1896 to produce the Yellow Kid for his *New York Journal*, the erstwhile *Hogan's Alley* was re-titled *McFadden's Row of Flats* in order to avoid a copyright dispute with Pulitzer, who continued publishing *Hogan's Alley*, now drawn by George Luks. This example is Outcault's second Yellow Kid production for Hearst. Like almost all of its predecessors at the *World*, the feature is essentially a humorous illustration, or single panel cartoon. Upon arrival at the *Journal*, Outcault's pictures began to be accompanied by a narrative text. Written by E. W. Townsend, author of a series of humorous albeit sentimental tales about slum children, the text seldom had much direct relationship to Outcault's picture, but by teaming the popular humor writer with the equally celebrated cartoonist, Hearst sought to enhance the appeal of his Sunday supplement and outsell Pulitzer's *World*. The enormous merchandising capacity of the character is alluded to in the box sign held aloft just above the Kid's head. Outcault occasionally referred to political issues in his cartoons but, as the sign over the Headquarters of the Juvenile Political Club indicates, the cartoonist took no sides: Bryan and McKinley did not share the ticket in the 1896 Presidential campaign; they were the opposing party candidates.

*Back cover:* Charles Schulz (Born 1922), **Snoopy as the Yellow Kid**. 1995. Collection of Mark J. Cohen and Rose Marie McDaniel. Copyright © 1995 United Feature Syndicate, Inc.

# Contents

This publication documents an exhibition held at the

FRYE ART MUSEUM

704 Terry Avenue, Seattle, Washington 98104

September 19 – November 8, 1998

and the

CARTOON ART MUSEUM

814 Mission Street, San Francisco, California 94103

November 21, 1998–February 21, 1999

Publication editor: Richard V. West

Copyeditor: Carole M. Levinthal

Publication design: N. Zaslavsky, Ultragraphics, Los Angeles, CA 90292

Publication distribution: University of Washington Press, P.O. Box 50096, Seattle, WA 98145

Printing: Typecraft, Inc., Pasadena, CA 91107

Photography: Susan Dirk/Under the Light

Library of Congress Cataloging-in-Publication Data
Harvey, Robert C.
        Children of the yellow kid  :  the evolution of the American comic
    strip / Robert C. Harvey  ;  with contributions by Brian Walker ,
    Richard V. West .
        p.    cm.
        Includes bibliographical references and index.
    1. Comic books, strips, etc. — United States — History and
    criticism.    I. Walker, Brian.    II. West, Richard V.    III. Title
    PN6725.H38   1998
    741.5'0973 — dc21                              98-40933
                                                      CIP

ISBN 0-295-97778-7

Manufactured in the United States of America.

# Acknowledgments

THE "HISTORY" OF THE AMERICAN comic strip is a lively one, but exceedingly brief—hardly over a century. While a great deal of attention is currently being bestowed upon the comics as they embark upon a second century, no such attention was paid to their inception a hundred years ago. Hence, much of the early saga of the "funny papers" has been shrouded in anecdote or clouded by the lack of factual information. Exact dates and events have been notoriously difficult to pin down with any certainty. We are indebted to Robert C. Harvey for his grasp of the history of the comic art form and his skill in researching the key moments and turning points in its evolution. As author, he has provided a concise and informative overview of major developments in the medium. As curator, he has selected images that counterpoint and parallel the issues discussed in the text. Taken together, words and images create a powerful and compelling message which we hope will be a major contribution to the appreciation of the comic strip form.

It takes the efforts of many to complete a complex project such as this one. While many examples of "narrative sequential art"—the comics—have been readily availible in print, reproduction of the original art work has been far less frequent. One of the major purposes of this book ( and the exhibition that initiated it) is to make available images of the original art work so that the unique achievements of the comics creators can be better understood. We are in debt to a number of institutions and individuals, beginning with the generous collectors and artists who graciously loaned works for display in the exhibition and inclusion in this book. In particular, we extend our thanks to Lucy Shelton Caswell, professor and curator of the Cartoon Research Library, Ohio State University; Mark J. Cohen and Rose Marie McDaniel; Trustee Mort Walker, past Director Kip Eagen, and Collections Coordinator Stephen Charla of the International Museum of Cartoon Art, Boca Raton; and Trustee Frank Norick, Executive Director Rod Gilchrist, and

Gallery Manager Dustin McGahan of the Cartoon Art Museum, San Francisco, for their help and encouragement during the organization of the exhibition.

I am also grateful to the members of the Frye Art Museum staff and volunteers who worked so diligently on all aspects of this project: David Andersen, MaryAnn Barron, Cathy Blackburn, Steven J. Broocks, Raymond P. Cox, Mark Eddington, Lilly Kassos, Anita Halstead, Brian J. Higdon, Sr., Alexa Hodson, Jack N. Hyder, Jr., Ann M. Jespersen, Carole M. Levinthal, Michelle Mehan, Kelly M. Myers, Neal E. Pedersen, Nannette F. Peterson, Kimsey S. Sorensen, and Roberta Stothart. Executive Assistant to the Director Roxanne M. Hadfield worked far beyond the call of duty to coordinate writing, editing, proofing, and the review of manuscripts and captions.

In conclusion, it seems fitting to honor here, also, those writers, critics, and scholars whose past publications and insights have helped establish our understanding of the history and prehistory of comics. Among them are Stephen Becker, Bill Blackbeard, Thomas Craven, Bill Crouch, Ron Goulart, David Kunzle, Richard Marschall, Scott McCloud, Jerry Robinson, Gilbert Seldes, Martin Sheridan, and Coulton Waugh.

And now for the second century.


Richard V. West, Executive Director

Frye Art Museum

## A Note on the Illustrations

The original art work for a published comic strip is normally photographed as a "line shot" that picks up only the black inked lines and areas. In order to present an accurate record of the appearance of the original art work, we have reproduced them in color, including those which would normally appear as black and white when seen in the daily newspaper. By doing this, we can show, for instance, not only the final published appearance in black-and-white of Walt Kelly's *Pogo*, but the blue pencil sketches that lie beneath the inked lines, thus giving an insight into Kelly's creative process. Similarly, the illustrations pick up faint black pencil lines in some examples that were not entirely erased before submitting the art work to the engraver. Also revealed are blemishes in the pictures—aged glue stains, for example, and different shades of paper where the cartoonist has pasted a piece of paper over the artwork in order to correct a drawing or some lettering. The more obvious of these seeming flaws in the originals are pointed out in the captions, but we make no reference (except with this note) to numerous small discolorations and blotches that appear in some of the reproductions. On these pages, then, you see the original art work of comic strips as it exists today, not as it appeared on the comics page of your daily newspaper.

# The State of the Art

BRIAN WALKER

ON OCTOBER 27, 1989, Bill Watterson, the creator of *Calvin and Hobbes,* gave a speech at the Ohio State University Festival of Cartoon Art entitled "The Cheapening of the Comics."

Watterson asked the audience: "Consider only the most successful strips in the paper today. Why are so many of them poorly drawn? Why do so many offer only the simplest interchangeable gags and puns? Why are some strips written by committees and drawn by assistants? Why are some strips still stumbling around decades after their original creators have retired or died? Why are some strips little more than advertisements for dolls and greeting cards? Why do so many of the comics look the same? If comics can be so much, why are we settling for so little? Can't we expect more from our comics pages?"

The following day Mort Walker, the creator of *Beetle Bailey,* addressed the same audience with a more optimistic outlook.

Walker countered Watterson by challenging the listeners: "Look at the comics page today. You don't have a stack of dopey jokes. You have a spread of human experiences, zapped with a humorous spark, a smorgasbord of life from politics to working women, to mothers with children, to people with pets, to pets with people, to all kinds of people with all kinds of other people. The comics page covers the whole gamut of life, and sometimes even extraterrestrial life. What a way to start the day! With a smile."

Is the current state of the art as dark as Watterson paints it or as bright as Walker colors it? Obviously, it is a matter of opinion. People who care about the comics get very passionate when they talk about their likes and dislikes. The truth lies somewhere in between. The funnies business has changed, for better or for worse, over the last 100 years. The fact that it has survived is beyond dispute. This publication and the exhibition that sparked it provide dramatic proof of the art form's evolution and resilience.

The comics have been under attack almost from the moment of their birth. Articles announcing the "death of the comics" first appeared in national periodicals at the turn of the century and have continued, without interruption, until today. In 1908, the *Boston Herald* reported, "The comic section has had its day. The funnies are not funny anymore and they have become vulgar in design and tawdry in color. We have had many protests come from the public against the continuance of the comic supplements. Parents and teachers object to them. Most discerning persons throw them aside without inspection, experience having taught them that there is no hope for improvement in these gaudy sheets."

A *Fortune* magazine article of 1933 claimed: "With the substitution of narrative interest in what is essentially a hit-and-run medium and with the further degeneration into the pictorial reproduction of cheaply romantic and sentimental stories, the comics have lost much of their old vitality."

A 1994 cover story entitled "The Decline and Fall of American Comics" was featured in *The National Review.* Writer Anthony LeJeune lamented the days when comics "created a common culture that, for a while, brought old and young, immigrants and native-born, together across the breakfast table, providing not only thrills and laughs but values identifiable with what would then have been a generally accepted concept of Americanism." LeJeune claimed that "nobody fights over the breakfast table for a first glimpse of *Calvin and Hobbes* or hurries to the street corner for the latest episode of *Cathy.*"

Some of our most prominent comics historians also offer a gloomy perspective on the art form's current state. In *America's Great Comic-Strip Artists* (1989), Richard Marschall states: "There have been many new comic strips but few trends since the 1950s, a situation that falls somewhere between sad and frightening. Commerce, once such a benign partner, today smothers the newspaper comic strip in America. Licensing and merchandising considerations now often precede the creation of a strip, rather than the reverse. Printing quality has declined, and coloring is not as brilliant as it once was. Formats have shrunk, and Sunday comics are now crowded several to a page instead of each filling a whole sheet. New features seem imitative; the gag-a-day mode has degenerated into stale punch lines; and newspapers themselves no longer promote—or evidently, appreciate—comic strips as they once did." In *The Comic Strip Century* (1995), Bill Blackbeard concludes that "by the 1960s, the newspaper comic strip had largely self-destructed as a measurably competent narrative art form."

By writing off the entire second half of the comic strip century, these eminent scholars overlook the contributions of great talents such as Walt Kelly, Charles Schulz, Garry Trudeau, Lynn Johnston, and

*opposite:* **2.** Richard Felton Outcault (1863-1928) and Archie Gunn (1863-1930). **American Humorist** (Sunday colored comic supplement for the *New York Journal*). December 6, 1896. Color tearsheet, 19¹/₂ × 14³/₄ in. (495 × 375 mm). Richard D. Olsen Collection, The Ohio State University Cartoon Research Library.

Several of the earliest covers of *American Humorist* combined the artwork of two of the publication's stellar attractions, cartoonist Outcault and pin-up artist Gunn. Outcault contributed a rendering of the Yellow Kid, and Gunn drew one of the showgirls with which he had been capturing the spirit of New York's emerging musical comedy stage.

Bill Watterson. The critics ignore the popularization of American comics around the world and the successful adaptation of newspaper comic strip creations to new media, such as television and computers.

The argument that comics have changed for the better is rarely made. Today, however, more minorities are represented on the funnies pages than ever before. Women cartoonists have established a voice and old taboos have tumbled. Cartoons are read by far more people than in the so-called "golden age" of the 1930s.

Doomsayers underestimate the art form's ability to reinvent itself. "I've read articles that were about to put us all out of business," said Milt Caniff in 1984. "And the next year some new thing like *Hagar the Horrible* comes along and knocks all of the pins down." The same could be said in more recent years for *Calvin and Hobbes* or *Dilbert.*

Obviously, the state of the art is a debatable issue. There is no question that the comics industry has changed dramatically throughout the past century. Radio, television, and digital media have challenged newspapers for dominance. Cartoonists have been forced to adapt to shifting perceptions and market conditions.

There will always be those who claim that comics were better back in the "good old days" in much the same way that sports fans discuss the merits of modern athletes versus former greats. Comparing Charles Schulz's influence *(Peanuts)* to George Herriman's genius *(Krazy Kat)* is as pointless as measuring Ken Griffey Jr.'s athletic ability against Babe Ruth's impact. They're different talents working in different eras.

An objective examination of how the funnies business has evolved over the course of the last century should enhance the appreciation of today's comics. In tracing the connections between contemporary creations and strips from the past, a deeper understanding can be achieved. I think if Bill Watterson had done his homework, he wouldn't have had such a one-sided point of view about the current state of the art.

Robert C. Harvey, author of this publication, is a comics scholar who does not subscribe to the "lost art" theory. The examples he has chosen to illustrate and his accompanying text provide dramatic proof that, although the American newspaper comic strip has changed over the past century, it still has a bright future ahead. Throughout its hundred-year history, the art form has, time and again, proven its popular appeal and commercial adaptability. From the newspaper wars at the end of the nineteenth century to the cutting edge competition on the information superhighway in the waning years of the twentieth century, comics have survived.

The funnies have endured primarily because comic strip characters have a universal, timeless appeal. Their daily appearances make them familiar to millions. Their struggles make them seem human. Their spirit makes them lovable. The comics have created friends for people as well as establishing a great cultural legacy. A smile is all they ask in the way of thanks. ●

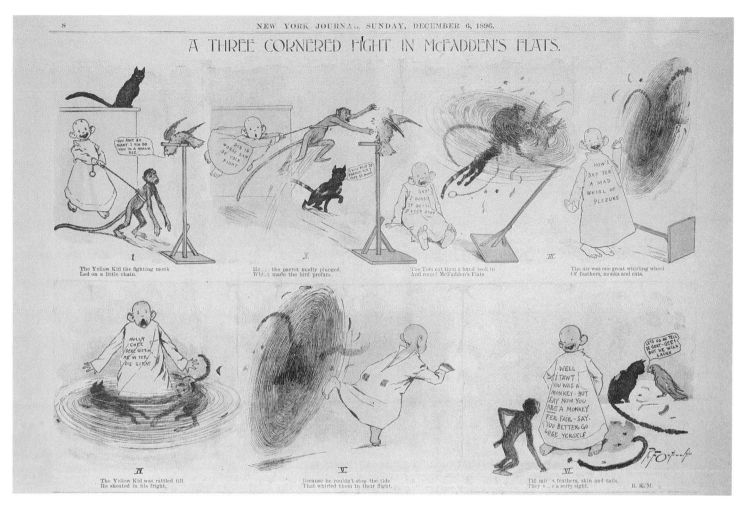

3. Richard Felton Outcault (1863-1928). **The Yellow Kid** (October 18, 1896 - January 23, 1898). December 6, 1896. Color tearsheet, 19¹/₂ × 14³/₄ in. (495× 375mm). Richard D. Olsen Collection, The Ohio State University Cartoon Research Library.

To capitalize on the appeal of the Yellow Kid, Outcault was directed to produce for the *American Humorist* a second feature every week in which the bald gamin would bask almost alone in the spotlight. And for this, the cartoonist resorted to a series of pictures in a humorous narrative sequence, a "comic strip," the first of which appeared October 25, 1896; this is the fourth of that series. Early comic strips were often accompanied by verbiage beneath the pictures.

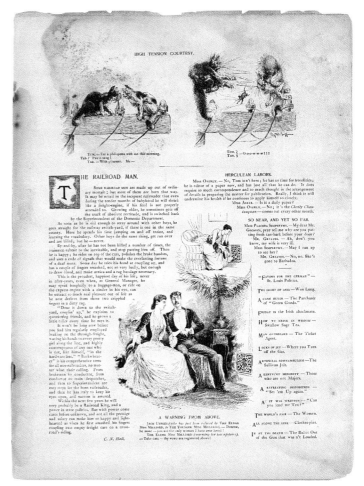

**4. Puck,** November 6, 1889 (pages 166 -167). Collection of Robert C. Harvey.

The newspaper Sunday comic supplements of the 1890s were established in imitation of the weekly humor magazines like *Puck, Life, and Judge*. These two pages from *Puck* are typical of the breed in the last decades of the nineteenth century. The humor was furnished by short prose fiction, verse, paragraphs (jokes), and drawings that illustrated dialogue printed beneath the pictures (e.g., "Needless Alarm"). In these "comic weeklies," the "comic strip" format was already in embryonic state with sequences of pictures that presented short comedic episodes (e.g.,"The Slot Movement" and "High Tension Courtesy").

# Children of the Yellow Kid: The Evolution of the American Comic Strip

IN THE BEGINNING, there were words appended to pictures, and the result was called "comics." But before we had the genuine article, the modern newspaper comic strip, the words and the pictures had to be integrated into a new art form: not just illustrated verbiage or footnoted pictures but an entirely different art form.

The evolution of the quintessential comic strip took less than a decade, but the form continued to evolve and mutate in minor but significant ways throughout its history. The growth of the medium through its first century can be outlined in five chapters or "movements," a more descriptive term perhaps, implying, to me at least, not just motion but a series of progressive developments that often overlap one another, each embracing past as well as present. Those five movements are identified in the headings that follow. And we begin, as most historical surveys of this medium do, with the Yellow Kid. ●

**YES! MRS. KATZENJAMMER WILL SAVE HER DARLING SONS.**
With a Club.

**5.** Rudolph Dirks (1877-1968), **The Katzenjammer Kids** (December 12, 1897-Present). December 23, 1900. Color tearsheet, 8 3/8 × 14 1/2 in. (213 × 368 mm). Richard D. Olsen Collection, The Ohio State University Cartoon Research Library.

The longest-running American comic strip, *The Katzenjammer Kids* is still being published. Essentially pantomimes, the earliest of the strips did not incorporate speech balloons within the drawings but were accompanied by text beneath the pictures, verbiage that was largely superfluous to an understanding of the action. Here, the speeches of the kids are needed to supply the reason for the mother's leaping to the table; her action makes little sense without the speeches, just as her speech in the last panel makes little sense without the picture. The page is fairly typical of early Sunday comics sections: the interior pages were sometimes printed in only two colors and often featured short verse or comic paragraphs in addition to cartoons.

## The Power of Character

Outcault discovered, like many have before and since, that creating a popular character confers upon the creator a mixed blessing. Writing about the Yellow Kid on May 1, 1898, he says: "By this time, the Yellow Kid had overwhelmed me. I dreamed of him…. I believe that I finally began to think that there was such a person as the Yellow Kid…. I look back on that fateful day [that my pen first traced the outlines of Mickey Dugan on paper], and it is hard to realize that not a sun has set since then that has not seen at least one more representation of the Yellow Kid reproduced. In that time, I suppose I have myself made twenty thousand Yellow Kids, and when the million buttons, the innumerable toys and cigarette boxes and labels and whatnot are taken into consideration, some idea can be gleaned of how tired I am of him. But the Yellow Kid will not separate himself from me, try as I may to make him, and I have given up my whole life to him." [2] Novelist Tom DeHaven wrote a fictionalized account of Outcault and his life with the Yellow Kid in *Funny Papers* (Viking, 1985).

# Origin of a New Species

## MOVEMENT I

BUT THE YELLOW KID wasn't the first comic strip, American or otherwise. Nor was the feature in which he appeared the first Sunday comic strip in color. (In fact, it wasn't even a "strip.") However, the Yellow Kid was the first comics character to demonstrate, beyond all question or quibble, the enormous appeal of the comics. Readers doted on the funnies. So the comics sold newspapers. That phenomenon gave the medium a future because it gave comics a mercantile basis. And if the distinction of the venerable Yellow Kid's having pioneered commercial success isn't sufficient justification for beginning with him, we can invoke what Coulton Waugh called the "Columbus Principle." Waugh's *The Comics,* published in 1947, was among the earliest sustained attempts at charting the history of the artform, and Waugh did a remarkable job of it. He has been proven mistaken about a few things since, but for the most part, he successfully identified the major developments in the growth of the medium and the key players in its history. In various places, Waugh was clearly using the Columbus Principle, which, he told us, works like this: the Vikings may have been the first Europeans to tread the beaches in the Western hemisphere, but Columbus inspired others with his visit and thereby gets all the credit.[1] Ditto the Yellow Kid.

The Yellow Kid was the inadvertent invention of Richard F. Outcault. Outcault lived in Flushing, New York, and made a living doing technical drawings for such periodicals as *Electric World,* but he also submitted cartoons to the weekly humor magazines, *Life, Puck, Judge,* and the somewhat more risque *Truth.* In 1894, the popularity of these comic magazines (or "comics," as they were usually called, a fateful slangy encryption) attracted the attention of Morrill Goddard, the Sunday editor of the *New York World.* He decided to piggyback on that popularity by producing a full-color Sunday supplement that would ape the humor magazines but would go them one better: the magazines did not use color extensively or with any great regularity. When Goddard started asking around for a comic artist to help provide the content for his brain child, Outcault was recommended to him. And when the supplement debuted November 18, 1894, it carried a full-page color comic strip by Outcault. In six consecutive wordless panels, Outcault traces the history of a clown and his dog on a picnic: when the dog is devoured by a huge snake, the gleeful clown cuts holes in the snake's belly for the dog's legs to emerge and leads the hybrid creature off. With unwitting prescience, Outcault titled this production "Origin of a New Species."

The *World's* November 1894 supplement was not the first Sunday newspaper supplement; nor was it the first supplement in color. But, concocted in deliberate imitation of the weekly humor magazines, it was apparently the first full-color "comics" supplement. (Yes, the term "comics" was forthwith applied to the Sunday supplement as well as to the weekly humor magazines that inspired it, thereby branding forever an embryonic art form with a name that would, in the fullness of time, become wholly inappropriate.) The strip format of Outcault's offering notwithstanding, most of the comics in the supplement were single-panel cartoons of the kind that appeared in *Judge* and *Life,* humorous drawings, often with multiple-speaker captions (that looked like dialogue in a play script) below the pictures. These were, in effect, illustrated verbal jokes. And the character destined to be christened the Yellow Kid first appeared in one of them.

Outcault had been doing cartoons about street urchins and tenement waifs for *Truth,* and the *World* reprinted one of these in the Sunday supplement of February 17, 1895, thus inadvertently establishing the date celebrated in some quarters as the birth of the comic strip. In this cartoon was a bald kid in a night-shirt. The kid made repeated appearances in Outcault's cartoons, the titles of which often included a reference to "Hogan's Alley" as their locale (the name borrowed from the opening line of "Maggie Murphy's Home," a popular song in a theatrical production of the day). The kid got a little taller and his ears got bigger and he acquired a gap-tooth grin. Then on January 5, 1896, his nightshirt was colored yellow. And people started calling him the Yellow Kid, discarding forever his real name, Mickey Dugan (FIGURE 1).

The Yellow Kid became popular enough that by the following fall William Randolph Hearst wanted Outcault to do the cartoon for him in his *New York Journal's* new weekly supplement, the *American Humorist* (FIGURE 2). Outcault had done about thirty Yellow Kid cartoons for Joseph Pulitzer's *World* when he was lured away to join the Hearst works: the first issue of the supplement appeared on October 18, 1896. Pulitzer gave the *Hogan's Alley* feature to another artist, George Luks, and Pulitzer and Hearst wooed readers with posters and promotions that splashed the Yellow Kid and his vacant grin all over New York, making the cartoon character the most conspicuous combatant in the press lords' battle for circulation.

*opposite:* **6.** James Swinnerton (1875-1974). **Little Jimmy** (February 14, 1904 intermittently until 1958). Sunday color guide, July 5, 1914. Traces of graphite, watercolor, pen and ink on illustration board, 19 3/4 × 14 3/4 in. (502 × 375 mm). Collection of the Cartoon Art Museum, San Francisco.

One of the three "founding fathers" of the American comic strip (with Outcault and Dirks), Swinnerton didn't create his most famous character until well after the comic strip form was established: he was the tiny tot who never got anything right in *Little Jimmy,* a comic strip that Swinnerton produced sporadically throughout his life. This strip was also a color guide for the newspaper's engraving department: by coloring every object the first time it appears (and only the first time, eschewing repetitive labor), Swinnerton told the engravers what color to make each object at every subsequent appearance.

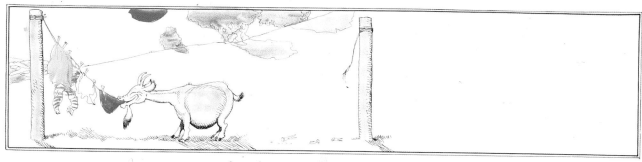

Those watching the warfare from the sidelines took to calling the two papers "the Yellow Kid journals," or "the yellow journals," and the kind of sensation-mongering journalism the warring papers practiced was thereafter dubbed "yellow journalism."

It was this struggle of the titans for circulation supremacy that demonstrated the commercial power of comics; and if we denominate the Yellow Kid as the progenitor of the species because of his appeal in the marketplace, perhaps we ought to have celebrated the centennial in 1996, commemorating his role in the competition for readership. But we didn't. History is a sloppy affair as it is being made: it's only hindsight that divides it into the familiar eras and epochs of textbooks, and the same backward glance landed on the merchandising prowess of the Yellow Kid and elevated him to prominence. So we stuck with custom.

But even as we tread here the beaten pathways to the medium's origins, we ought to recognize that newspaper comics were not invented by a single intelligence; nor did they appear all at once. And the Yellow Kid was not, really, the first of the lot. In Chicago, for instance, the *Inter Ocean* was publishing for young people in its Sunday supplement a full-page color cartoon about the doings of the Ting Ling Kids (by Charles W. Saalburg) as early as May 1894, well before anything Outcault did for the *World*. In every technical respect, Saalburg's cartoon was the equivalent of Outcault's Yellow Kid series, but it created no commercially viable excitement as the Yellow Kid did in New York.

Plainly, the ingredients of the newspaper comic strip were accruing in various places and under diverse hands during the last decade of the nineteenth century. The esteemed Waugh, looking back on this period with the benefit of mid-twentieth century perspective, defined comics in terms of their mature form. Comics, he said, embrace three elements: (1) a narrative sequence of pictures in which (2) speech balloons are included in the drawings, the combination showcasing (3) a character or characters who reappear with each publication of the feature. This last quality seems to me to be somewhat trumped up. The first two aspects of the medium are rooted in its form; the third refers to content. Clearly, a narrative sequence of pictures in which the characters speak by blurting out what they have to say in puffs of dialogue called "speech balloons" is a comic strip whether or not the characters appear again and again. The character qualification was probably tacked on in order to eliminate all the predecessors to the Yellow Kid.

The importance of speech balloons in the art form cannot be overestimated. Speech balloons breathe into comic strips their peculiar life. In all other graphic representations, characters are doomed to wordless posturing and pantomime—but in comic strips, they speak. And their speeches are made in the same mode

( CONTINUED PAGE 27 )

*opposite:* **7.** Frederick Burr Opper (1857-1937). **Happy Hooligan** (March 11, 1900-April 7, 1918; January 1927-August 14, 1932). Sunday color guide, 1909. Traces of graphite, watercolor, pen and ink on illustration board, 25 3/4 x 20 1/2 in (654 x 521 mm). Collection of Mark J. Cohen and Rose Marie McDaniel.

This installment of Opper's *Happy Hooligan* is a good example of the interdependence of word and picture in the comic strip form: the humor depends upon our comprehending the meaning of both the verbal and the visual content, neither of which, alone without the other, is as funny. In fact, here the unpleasant nature of Happy's new circus "act" is revealed only in the pictures; and the comic irony of the outcome of this hazardous venture is revealed only in the circus manager's speeches; and it is the coupling of these two revelations that creates the comedy.

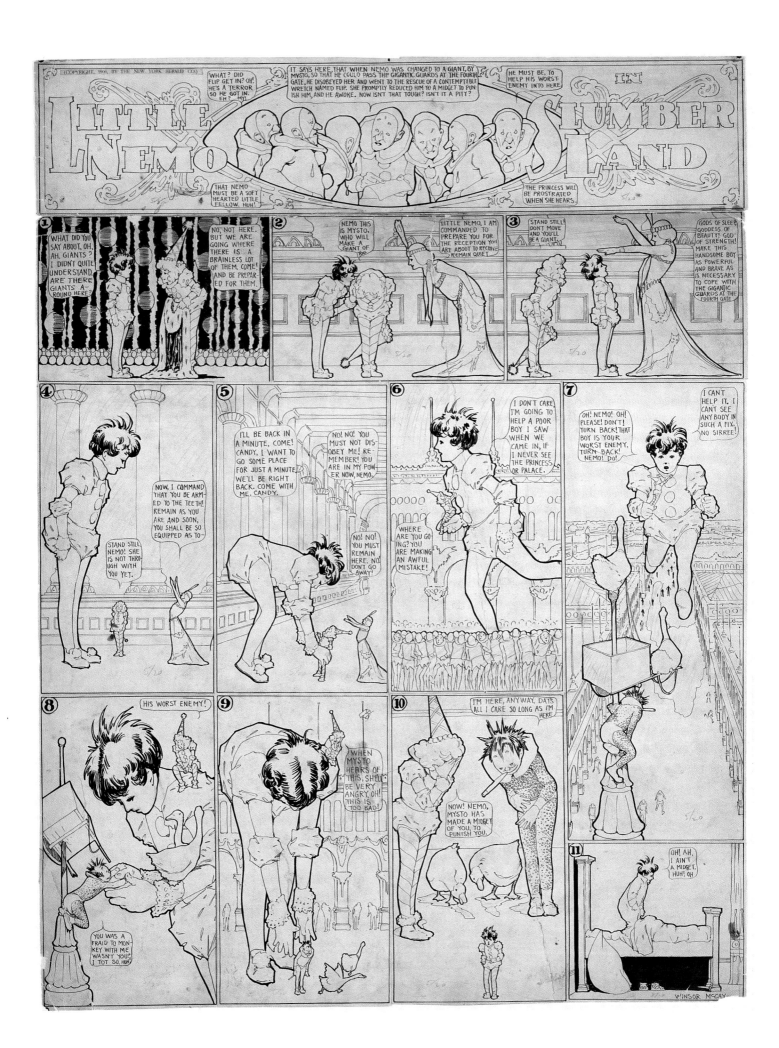

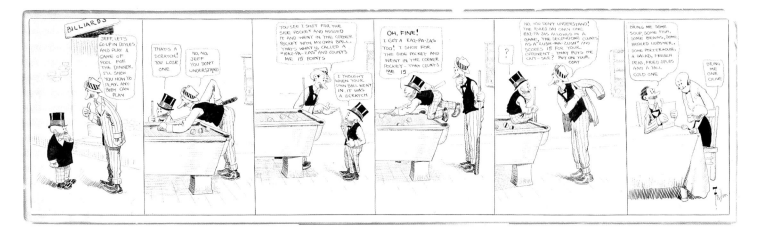

**9.** Bud Fisher (1884 -1954), **Mutt and Jeff** (November 15, 1907 - June 25, 1983). About 1911. Traces of graphite, pen and ink on illustration board, 7 1/8 × 26 in. (181 × 660 mm). Collection of Jim Scancarelli.

Beginning as a "one joke" sports page feature called *A. Mutt* that described the fortunes and misfortunes of a habitual gambler, Fisher's creation changed with the arrival of little Jeff, fugitive from an insane asylum, who gave the strip its humanity. Jeff's seeming mental deficiency made him the perfect innocent, the ideal foil for Mutt the conniving materialist. Although Jeff is frequently the victim of Mutt's scheming, the tall guy's plans are just as often upset by the little fellow's benign ignorance. And the readers rooted for Jeff: the short guy is visually the underdog, always the American favorite. Jeff in his gentleness is also the more appealing of the two personalities. In an unwitting self-revelation, Fisher once confessed to liking Mutt best.

*opposite:* **8.** Winsor McCay (1867 - 1934), **Little Nemo in Slumberland** (October 15, 1905 - July 23, 1911). May 20, 1906. Traces of blue pencil and graphite, pen and ink on illustration board, 28 × 21 1/2 in. (711 × 546 mm). Philip Sills Collection, The Ohio State University Cartoon Research Library.

The medium's first authentic genius, McCay exercised a pervasive sense of design as he explored the potential of the comic strip form in ways few had attempted before—and none did again for at least two decades after the first run of *Little Nemo.* For instance, McCay varied the size and shape of his panels to give visual emphasis to the narrative he was depicting: the verticality of the shapes here dramatizes Nemo's size.

gotta hand it to Jeff. By Bud Fisher.

**10.** Bud Fisher (1884 -1954), **Mutt and Jeff** (November 15, 1907 - June 25, 1983), September 24, 1918. Blue pencil, pen, and ink on illustration board, 8 3/4 x 27 3/4 in. (222 x 705 mm). Philip Sills Collection, The Ohio State University Cartoon Research Library.

During World War I, Mutt and Jeff joined the American Expeditionary Force. Fisher was also in uniform, drawing the strip on weekends in a hotel room near wherever he was stationed. The cartoonist had enlisted because the war promised to be a "big show," as he put it, and since he'd seen most of the other "shows," he figured he might as well "take it in." But he planned to continue producing his comic strip and when the American army brass forbade it, Fisher transferred to the British army. Commissioned a captain, he was attached to the Censor Publicity Bureau of General Headquarters and spent several months along the Western Front in France where he "got lots of grand material" that turned up in the strip as horseplay of the kind seen here. The blue pencil shading indicates to the engravers where to add a Ben-Day dot pattern to produce the visual effect of gray. (Light blue does not photograph in the engraving process.) A penciled notation written over the strip on the original artwork, "As a sand-bag dropper, you gotta hand it to Jeff," comments on the action in the strip. Set in type, many newspapers published the "overline" as a subtitle for the day's installment. The practice, which was once as much a part of every daily comic strip as pictures and speech balloons, was discontinued shortly after World War II.

## Fisher the Trail Blazer

Fisher did more for the comic strip medium than establish its format. According to John Wheeler, founder of the Wheeler (later Bell) Syndicate (distributor of *Mutt and Jeff* for most of its run), Fisher, "by his guts and independence, probably did more to make the cartoon business for his more cowardly confreres than anyone else who has ever been in it." Before *A. Mutt* was a month old, Hearst had lured Fisher away from the *Chronicle* to the *Examiner;* but before Fisher left, he took care to copyright the strip in his name. Waiting until after his editor approved the day's strip, Fisher went into the engraving room and before the plate was made, wrote "Copyright 1907, H. C. Fisher" in the corner of the last strip the *Chronicle* published.[9] Later (in November 1914), Fisher registered the name "Mutt and Jeff" as a trademark, and when he left Hearst for Wheeler in 1915, he won the ensuing legal battle over rights to the name.

And Fisher's fights for his rights as a cartoonist were not confined to the courtroom. Stephen Becker tells us that while Fisher was still a staff cartoonist for the *Chronicle,* the paper reduced the size allotted to his cartoon without consulting him. Peeved, Fisher calmly tore up his artwork and refused to draw in the smaller dimension. In effect, he quit. But since he was obliged to give two weeks' notice, he came to the office every day for the next week or so. He did not, however, touch pen or paper. After several days of this, his editor relented, and Fisher's cartoon resumed at its usual size.[10]

**11.** Bud Fisher (1884-1954), **Mutt and Jeff** (November 15, 1907-June 25, 1983). June 23, 1983. Traces of graphite, pen and ink on illustration board, 3³/₄ × 12¹/₄ in. (95 × 311 mm). Collection of Jim Scancarelli. Copyright © 1983 A Edita S. de Beaumont.

In its final years, *Mutt and Jeff* was produced by George Breisacher, assisted by Jim Scancarelli, who drew the strip. Occasionally—as in the case at hand—Scancarelli wrote gags, too. About this strip, Scancarelli said, "I wrote and drew this one all by myself, and two days later, *Mutt and Jeff* came to an end." He'd been working on the strip for over a year, and when he subsequently inherited *Gasoline Alley* in 1986, he became the only cartoonist to have worked on two strips in their seventy-fifth years.

as the rest of the strip—the visual mode. We see both the characters and what they say. Thus, including speech balloons within the pictures gives the words and the pictures concurrence—the lifelike illusion that the characters we see are speaking even as we see them, just as we simultaneously hear and see people in real life (FIGURE 3).

If speech balloons give comic strips their life, then breaking the narrative into successive panels gives that life duration, an existence beyond a moment. This breakdown of the action is to comics what time is to life. In fact, "timing"—pace as well as duration—is the direct result of sequencing pictures to make up a comic strip.

By the 1890s, the ingredients for the comic strip form had been around for a while, but it was the newspaper cartoonist who combined them all to create a durable new form. Waugh allows that the winning combination did not appear all at once but accumulated through the efforts of three individuals during the 1890s. First came continuing characters: Outcault in New York with the Yellow Kid in 1895; James Swinnerton in San Francisco with his little bears. Swinnerton devised a little bear cub (eventually called Baby Monarch) in the image of California's state symbol to promote interest in the Midwinter Exposition in the weeks before it opened in San Francisco in January 1894. Swinnerton's little bears appeared in the *San Francisco Examiner* day after day for quite some time. They were so popular that, even after the Exposition closed, they continued to appear in the "weather ears" at the top of the front page where they suggested the coming weather by wearing coats or swim suits or by carrying umbrellas. Reappearing characters like the Yellow Kid and the little bears captured a loyal readership, which, in turn, helped to establish the importance of cartoon features to newspaper sales.

Outcault was the first to employ a narrative sequence of pictures according to Waugh, but this is one of the instances of his being mistaken. "Strips" of narrative pictures had appeared in numerous forums well before Outcault's tenure with Pulitzer. In the weekly humor magazines, cartoonists resorted with some frequency to comic sequences rather than single panels (FIGURE 4). These strips were strictly pantomime ventures although sometimes narrative (but not speeches) appeared beneath the panels. In any case, Outcault didn't use the multiple-panel format for every appearance of the Yellow Kid. Reportedly, Rudolph Dirks was the first to use it regularly in his *Katzenjammer Kids,* which began December 12, 1897. At first, the antics of these mischievous juveniles were depicted silently; gradually, Dirks introduced verbal content—first, as a series of phrases under the panels, then in speech balloons (FIGURE 5). Eventually, Dirks routinely made speech balloons a fundamental aspect of the form. (Speech balloons had been employed occasionally by Outcault, too—and by other cartoonists as far back as the 18th century in Thomas Rowlandson's cartoon version of British society.)

By the turn of the century, the form as defined by Waugh had taken shape. The Sunday comics in color were a reality. Narrative sequences of pictures with speech balloons giving "visual voice" to the characters, the funnies in newspapers had assimilated facets of cartooning from other media and had emerged in a form now distinctly different from that of their brethren in humor magazines (FIGURE 6). Frederick Opper may have been the first to deploy all of the art form's resources at once with the debut of his *Happy Hooligan* strip in March 1900.

Opper was in many respects the greatest cartoonist of his generation, the only one to achieve success in all three forms of the art being practiced during his lifetime: magazine panel cartoon, editorial cartoon, and comic strip. Born in 1857 in Madison, Ohio, he quit school at the age of fourteen to work in the village store; after a few months, he went to work as a printer's devil for the local weekly newspaper. While there, he learned to set type. Always drawing "comical sketches," he decided about a year later to go to New York where so many of the comic weeklies were published.

As he recounted the experience in Orison Sweet Marden's *Little Visits with Great Americans:* "My self-esteem was not so great as to rate myself a full-fledged artist. My idea was to obtain a position as a compositor in New York, to draw between times, and gradually to land myself where my hopes all centered."[3] Unhappily, he discovered that to be a compositor, he would have to apprentice himself for three years.

( CONTINUED PAGE 32 )

*opposite:* **12.** George McManus (1884-1954), **Bringing Up Father** (January 2, 1913-Present). Sunday color guide, May 9, 1920. Watercolor, pen and ink on illustration board, 21½ × 16½ in. (546 × 419 mm.). Collection of Mark J. Cohen and Rose Marie McDaniel.

Many early strips were single-theme (or "one joke") enterprises like McManus's masterpiece that pitted the unaffected low-brow desires of Jiggs against his wife Maggie's vaulting social pretensions in an epic comedy of husband-and-wife strife that would outlast its creator. Noted for the elegance of his sense of design and the delicacy of his line, the Irish cartoonist reveals the persistence of some of the traditional visual symbols of his craft--notably, the simian visage caricaturing an Irishman for his protagonist and a painfully homely face for Jiggs' wife, who is intended merely to be plain-looking.

*Maggie & Jiggs send all best wishes to the Harris family; Marilyn, Ron, Debbi & Jimmy.*

**13.** George McManus (1884-1954), **Bringing Up Father** (January 2, 1913-Present). November 2, 1943. Traces of graphite, blue pencil, pen and ink on illustration board, 5 1/8 × 17 1/8 in. (130 × 454 mm). Collection of Mark J. Cohen and Rose Marie McDaniel. Copyright © 1943. Reprinted with special permission of King Features Syndicate.

McManus's deft variation on his usual theme is enhanced by the decorative filigree of his linework in this sample of his mature style. Many of the feature's visual leitmotifs appear here—Jiggs' tightwire escape route, his top hat and cane, Maggie's spindly pet dog, and the picture on the wall in which a dancer blithely ignores the boundaries of the picture frame. Below McManus's signature is that of his long-time assistant, Zeke Zekley. Zekley frequently came up with jokes, and when McManus used

them, he would give Zekley what he called "a plus" (meaning that the signature on the strip that day would be "+ Zeke Zekley"). This addendum seldom was published, however, because the syndicate, saying that they were paying for the work of McManus (a celebrity) not that of Zekley (an unknown underling), instructed engravers to eliminate Zekley's name when producing plates and matts for distribution to client newspapers. Zekley, who was with McManus from the mid-1930s until the cartoonist died in 1954, worked side-by-side with his boss, and they passed the artwork back and forth between them, sharing equally in the drawing chores for most of the two decades they worked together. Although it was widely assumed that Zekley would inherit the strip, the syndicate, unaccountably, hired someone else.

*opposite:* **14.** George Herriman (1880-1944), **Krazy Kat** (October 28, 1913 - June 25, 1944). May 2, 1943. Traces of graphite, pen and ink on illustration board, 22 1/4 × 14 1/2 in. (565 × 368 mm). Charles H. Kuhn Collection, The Ohio State Cartoon Research Library. Copyright © 1943. Reprinted with special permission of King Features Syndicate.

*Krazy Kat* may be the ultimate in "one joke" strips. The emblematic brick in the strip was at first simply the equivalent of the vaudevillian's pie-in-the-face, a corrective administered to a miscreant partner on stage. But Herriman, through endless repetitions of the gesture, transcended pie and created a paean to love. In his eternal triangle, the Kat loves Ignatz the mouse, Ignatz scorns Krazy, and Offissa Pupp, instead of attacking the Kat, loves her (or "it," Krazy being sexless, like an elf or sprite). Ignatz expresses his disdain by throwing a brick at the Kat, which Krazy, blind with love, inter-

prets as a "missil [sic] of affection." Ironically, in seeking to protect the object of his passion from these assaults, Offissa Pupp succeeds in making his beloved Krazy happy only when he fails to frustrate Ignatz's attack. Luckily, Offissa Pupp fails often. And Ignatz, perforce, succeeds. But it is Krazy who prevails. As the critic Gilbert Seldes once wrote, "The incurable romanticist, Krazy faints daily in full possession of his illusion, and Ignatz, stupidly hurling his brick, thinking to injure, fosters the illusion and keeps Krazy 'heppy'." Hence, Herriman's theme: love always triumphs. Herriman deployed the resources of his medium with fanciful abandon: the desert scenery often changed from panel to panel, and on his Sunday pages, the layouts varied wildly and were often constructed expressly to create the gag. The joke here is enriched with the simultaneity afforded by the last panel's panoramic view, in which we read of Offissa Pupp's self-satisfaction while also realizing that he is failing in his mission even as he describes it.

5-2

So he found a job making window cards and other advertisements for a store. "All the leisure I had to myself," he continued, "evenings and holidays, I spent making comic sketches, and I took them to the comic papers—to the *Phunny Phellow* and *Wild Oats.* I just submitted rough sketches. Soon the editors permitted me to draw the [final] sketches also, which was a great encouragement." [4]

After eight or ten months of this, he was able to make a living cartooning, and he left the store to submit cartoons and drawings to *Wild Oats, Harper's Weekly, Frank Leslie's,* and *Century* among others. In 1877, he joined *Leslie's* as a staff artist on salary, and three years later, he left for *Puck,* where he did both political cartoons and humorous ones, until he landed at Hearst's *Journal* in 1899. He continued drawing hard-hitting editorial cartoons, and on March 11, 1900, he began producing his longest-lasting creation, *Happy Hooligan,* a Sunday comic strip about a pathetic but ludicrous Irish hobo with a tin can for a hat, who could be relied upon to lose at every opportunity (FIGURE 7). Happy was the perpetual fall guy, "a favorite son of misfortune," as Opper said; his fate was to have his good intentions forever frustrated by accident or ineptitude, inevitably ending each installment in physical discomfort.

Opper created many cartoon features thereafter (including *And Her Name Was Maud!* about a trouble-making mule, and *Alphonse and Gaston,* whose title characters were so excessively polite as to become a national catch-phrase), but *Happy Hooligan* lasted longest, ending August 14, 1932. Opper also illustrated some books, among them, humorist Bill Nye's *Comic History of the U.S.* in 1894. Opper was the first president of the Cartoonists Club, which started in the late 1920s. He was also the last president of the group. While all the members could agree that Opper's age, tenure, and professional stature entitled him to the honor, they could not agree on a successor. As Moses Koenigsberg tells it (in *King News):* "[The society] crashed into as many fragments as there were members. Each was of the unalterable conviction that he merited the chieftancy." [5]

Opper used the comic strip form pretty much as he found it. And he found it in the colored Sunday supplement. The next step in the evolution of the medium would result in establishing the daily "strip" format. And that was done by Harry Conway "Bud" Fisher in 1907. ●

# Fine-tuning the Form
# and Widening the Focus

## MOVEMENT 2

FISHER'S STRIP WAS NOT THE FIRST to be published daily on a regular basis; that distinction probably belongs to Clare Briggs, whose *A. Piker Clerk* ran daily for awhile in 1903 in the *Chicago American.* But Briggs' strip didn't last; Fisher's did. Again, Waugh's Columbus Principle applies. Until Fisher's *Mutt and Jeff* set the fashion, cartoons in the daily newspaper usually appeared as collections of comic drawings grouped almost haphazardly within the ruled border of a large single-frame panel. And these were most often found on the sports pages where they offered graphic reportage and humorous comment on the doings of diamond, ring, track, and other arenas of athletic competition. In 1907, Fisher was a sports cartoonist on the *San Francisco Chronicle.* Not surprisingly, the comic strip that became *Mutt and Jeff* started on the sports page and concerned a preoccupation of the sporting reader: betting.

Called *A. Mutt* at first, the strip focussed on the wagering adventures of a skinny racetrack tout. The inaugural strip appeared on November 15, 1907, and it was something of a departure from the usual sports cartoon of the day. Instead of grouping all his comic drawings into a single commodious square panel, Fisher spread his funny pictures across the width of the sports page in a narrow page-wide strip (as in FIGURE 9). His editor's consent to this venture was not as easily obtained as we might today suppose. John P. Young had turned down Fisher's suggestion for a sports page strip two years earlier because, he is alleged to have said, "it would take up too much room, and readers are used to reading down the page and not horizontally." [6]

But once Young had agreed to this experiment, the comic "strip" format was on its way to becoming a fixture in daily newspapers. Fisher scarcely imagined, however, that he was establishing an art form. "In selecting the strip form for the picture," he once wrote, "I thought I would get a prominent position

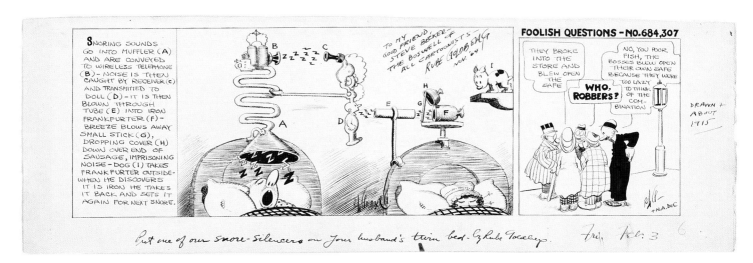

**15.** Rube Goldberg (1883-1970), **Inventions of Prof. Butts** (about 1909-1935). February 3, 1915. Pen and ink on illustration board, 5 1/8 × 17 in. (130 × 432 mm). Collection of Mark J. Cohen and Rose Marie McDaniel.

Goldberg's long career embraced every form of newspaper cartooning—one panel "anthology" humor on sports pages, comic strips, and single panel gags as well as editorial cartoons. Much of his early work is of the "one joke" variety (*Foolish Questions*, for instance), including the feature for which he was most famous, the inventions cartoon. In these, Goldberg indulged his suspicion that maybe modern technology wasn't all it purported to be, earning a place in the dictionary for his name to describe "extremely intricate diagrams of contraptions designed to effect relatively simple results" (*American Heritage Dictionary*).

across the top of the sporting page, which I did, and that pleased my vanity. I also thought the cartoon would be easy to read in this form. It was." [7]

The co-star of Fisher's feature, little Jeff, didn't appear until March 27, 1908. At the time, Mutt is sent to an insane asylum as a gambling addict, and meets Jeff there. Jeff is an inmate at the institution because he imagines that he is the heavyweight boxing champion, James Jeffries. Jeff faded from view pretty fast after his debut, but Fisher brought him back repeatedly over the next two years, and by 1910, the little fella was Mutt's regular foil although his name didn't appear in lights over the strip until 1916. By then, the "strip" format for daily cartoons in newspapers was firmly established.

By then, too, comic strips had bred a great variety of genre, widening the focus of the medium to embrace virtually every aspect of American life. At first, as we've seen, cartoonists concentrated on sports and kids. And the comics they produced generated a certain kind of censure. The disapproval arose partly because the weekly supplements were published on Sunday, the day of rest and religion. This criticism was further inflamed by the focus of the funnies. The world of sports was often infected with gamblers and other undesirables, and the Yellow Kid and his unkempt tenement-dwelling companions or the Katzenjammer Kids with their often vicious pranks weren't very good examples for their supposed reading audience, middle class children. These specimens of the cartoonist's craft were "as vulgar in design as they are tawdry in color" according to the critics.[11] Before long, however, cartoonists began peering into other facets of daily life, and as less objectionable subjects came in for scrutiny, the criticism faded (although it would never, ever, disappear entirely).

**16.** Milt Gross (1895-1953), **Dave's Delicatessen ("That's My Pop!")** (February 1931- about 1935). June 9, 1935. Traces of graphite, pen and ink on illustration board, 16 1/2 × 23 1/2 in. (419 × 597 mm). Collection of Mark J. Cohen and Rose Marie McDaniel. Copyright © 1935 Press Publishing Co.

Like many early newspaper cartoonists, Gross produced a variety of often short-lived single theme features, each based upon a catch phrase ("banana oil!" being one of them, an expression the equivalent of "baloney"). *Dave's Delicatessen,* one of his last efforts in this tradition, rehearsed for readers the comic blunderings of the good-hearted Dave. Rendered in a lunatic style that could well exemplify the "cartooning" manner of the first quarter of the century, the strip invariably ended with a somewhat extraneous panel in which Dave's scion, unaffected by the obvious incompetence of his father, proclaims triumphantly, "That's My Pop!" This final panel eventually became a stand-alone single panel feature, replacing Dave and inspiring a radio program in the 1940s.

**17.** Virginia Huget (1900-1991), **Molly the Manicure Girl** (1928-29). August 8, 1928. Blue pencil, pen, and ink on illustration board, 5 × 18 in. (127 × 457 mm). Charles H. Kuhn Collection, The Ohio State Cartoon Research Library. Copyright © 1928 Premier Syndicate, Inc.

Molly was one of several "flapper girl" strips engendered by the Jazz Age spirit, and Huget was one of several female cartoonists who depicted the emergence of the more liberated women of that period in their strips.

*Buster Brown* helped. Outcault eventually abandoned the Yellow Kid and his scruffy lower-class cohorts for a more respectable protagonist, whose adventures he started to record on May 4, 1902. Dressed in a Little Lord Fauntleroy outfit, Buster Brown was a mischievous kid, but he was regularly punished for his transgressions, and the weekly strip routinely concluded with a moral lesson. Little Nemo was another of the same class, but Nemo was a model citizen from the beginning.

Dreaming his adventures, Nemo awoke in the last panel of every Sunday installment. His dreams were sumptuous visual feasts, filled with strange creatures and places, exotic islands and palaces awe-inspiring in their glittering splendor and copious detail, all depicted with superb draftsmanship by the medium's earliest genius, Winsor McCay (FIGURE 8). Beginning October 15, 1905, *Little Nemo in Slumberland* was a stunning series of full-page productions in color, so masterfully produced that their like would not be seen again in the comics for another generation.

Comic strips about children proliferated throughout the history of the medium—Swinnerton's *Little Jimmy* (May 29, 1904), Lyonel Feininger's *The Kin-der-Kids* (April 29, 1906), Merrill Blosser's *Freckles and His Friends* (September 20, 1915), Gene Byrnes's *Reg'lar Fellas* (c. 1916, FIGURE 33), R. M. Brinkerhoff's *Little Mary Mixup* (1917), Edwina Dumm's *Cap Stubbs and Tippie* (early 1918, FIGURE 32), and Ernie Bushmiller's *Nancy* (who took Fritzi Ritz's place as the title character of the strip in the fall of 1938, FIGURE 38). Some of the kids were teenagers—Carl Ed's *Harold Teen* was probably the first (May 14, 1919); then came Paul Robinson's *Etta Kett* (c. 1925), and finally, Marty Links' *Bobby Sox* November 20, 1944 (FIGURE 48).

The family was also a focus. *Bringing Up Father* (January 2, 1913) was one of a series of strips that George McManus produced about married life in the first decade of the century (FIGURE 12).

(CONTINUED PAGE 46)

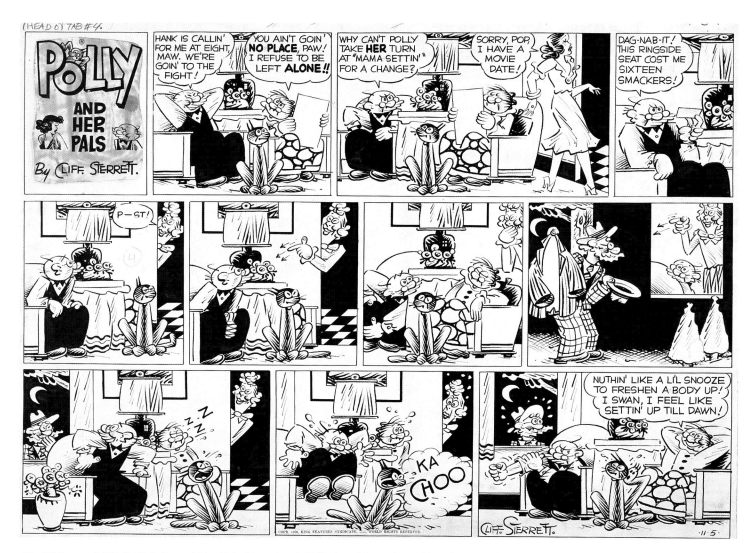

**18.** Cliff Sterrett (1883-1964), **Polly and Her Pals** (December 4, 1912 - June 15, 1958). November 5, 1950. Traces of blue pencil and graphite, pasteover, pen and ink on illustration board, 17 × 24 7/8 in. (432 × 632 mm). Charles H. Kuhn Collection, The Ohio State Cartoon Research Library. Copyright © 1950. Reprinted with special permission of King Features Syndicate.

Launched as *Positive Polly*, Sterrett's strip was ostensibly about the "new woman" of the century's second and subsequent decade, but the cartoonist soon focused on the collision of mores and custom between Polly and her Victorian father. More significant by far than the subject of the strip was Sterrett's graphic technique. Evocative of French cubism and Italian futurism, Sterrett's abstraction of human anatomy was surrounded by a riot of contrasting patterns—checks, stripes, solids, and geometric shapes of all sorts. The title panel here reflects a common practice: cartoonists usually had the strip's title printed separately in multiple copies and then clipped and pasted them on the Sunday strip illustration board.

**19.** Thomas A. Dorgan ("Tad") (1877-1929), **Judge Rummy's Court** (about 1911-1929). October 19, 1926. Traces of graphite, pen and ink on illustration board, 8 × 12 ½ in. (203 × 318 mm). Collection of the Cartoon Art Museum, San Francisco. Copyright © 1926 International Feature Service, Inc.

Although Tad began cartooning on the sports pages in San Francisco newspapers around 1900, by the time he got to New York in the second decade of the century, his *Indoor Sports* and *Outdoor Sports* cartoons were making social comment.

Tad was soon producing such comic strips as *Silk Hat Harry's Divorce Suit* and *Judge Rummy's Court* (seen here), both "funny animal" strips in which the the animals' wry adventures looked askance at the society around them. Populated with fighters, managers, actors, touts, and broken-down hangers-on, his panels often commented on life generally, and in them, he invented or popularized many catch phrases, such as "Yes, we have no bananas," "cheaters" (spectacles), "skimmer" (hat), and "cackle berries" (eggs).

**20.** J.R. Williams (1888-1957), **Out Our Way** (December 21, 1922-Present). November 12, 1932. Traces of graphite, pasteover, brush, pen and ink on illustration board, 11 × 12 in. (279 × 305 mm). Robert Ray Metz Collection, The Ohio State University Cartoon Research Library. Copyright © 1932. OUT OUR WAY reprinted by permission of Newspaper Enterprise Association, Inc.

Williams' folksy human interest panel cartoon (which appeared as a comic strip on Sundays) ruminated on the trials and tribulations, triumphs and tragedies, of everyday life in the machine shop, on the open range, and at home, as here in "Why Mothers Get Gray."

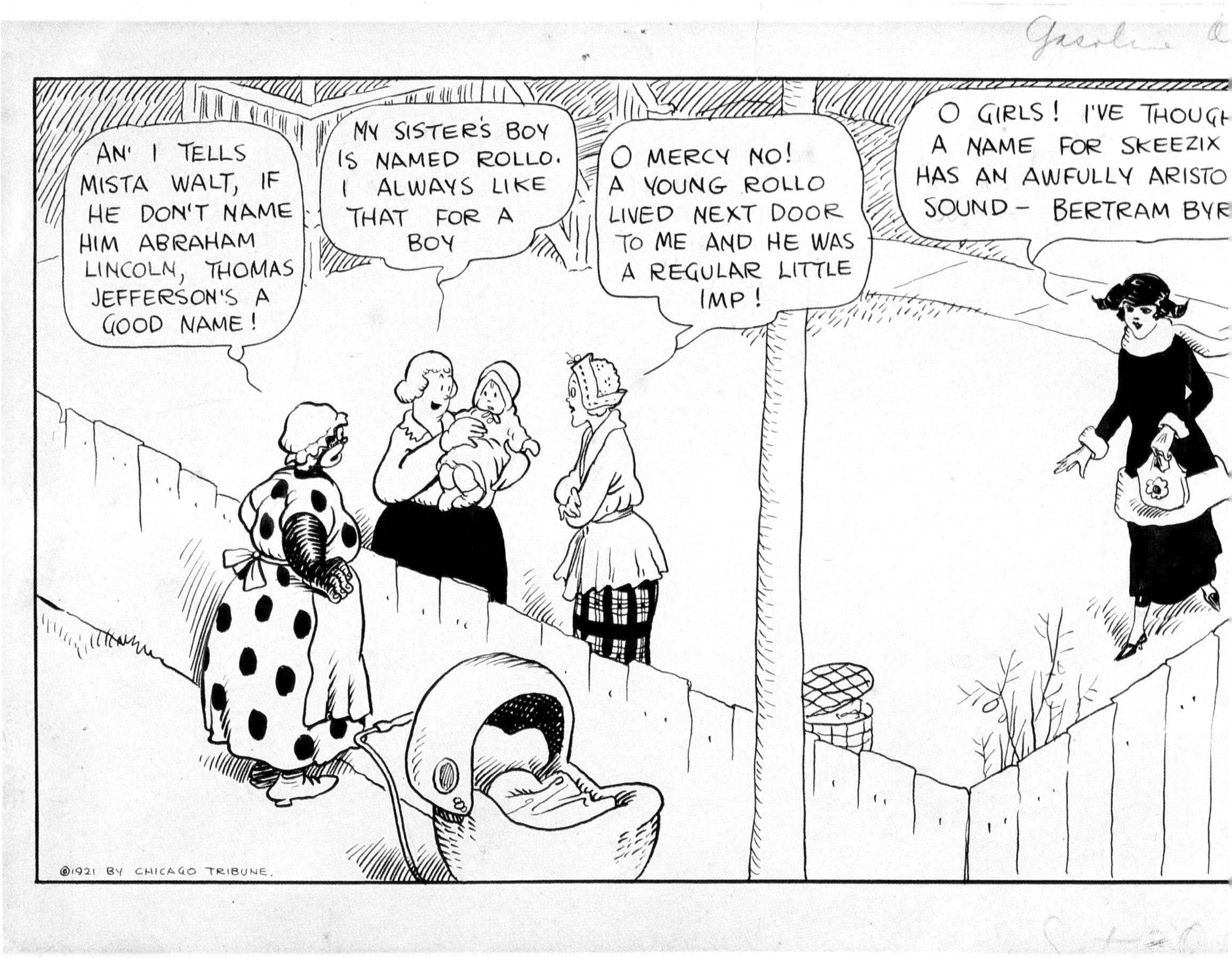


*see page 42:* **21.** Frank King, **Gasoline Alley**

To Bob Zschiesche, right hand man:
Here's wishing you a lot of fun in your car. - Frank O.
King - 1954.

King's strip was set firmly in small town America and in the alleys where men tinkered with their cars. When a baby boy was left on the doorstep of one of the would-be mechanics, Walt Wallet, the strip shifted from car fads to child-rearing and other family concerns. This installment recalls the feature's beginnings as a single panel cartoon, which evolved into strip format by the summer of 1920 (here, King "divides" the strip-wide panel into two segments by strategic placement of a telephone pole). Bob Zschiesche, to whom this strip is inscribed by King, was one of his assistants.

Although King's drawing style might appear somewhat pedestrian, his treatment of Sunday pages in the 1930s was often striking. Here, King imposed a grid of panel borders upon a single picture of a house under construction. The grid creates individual panels of various aspects of the scene, highlighting those aspects as focal points for the duration of a single panel. In autumn, King sometimes created spectacular visual treatments of the fall colors, once imitating German woodcut style.

## A Succession of Talent

An unusual aspect of *Gasoline Alley* resides in the succession of cartoonists who have produced it. Most comic strip features, concoctions unique to the individual creative sensibilities of those who first invent them, do not survive the departure of their creators. When Frank King retired in 1960, his creation was turned over to two of his assistants—Dick Moores, who continued the daily strip, and Bill Perry, who produced the Sunday page (FIGURE 23). Moores, in particular, was a remarkable successor. He maintained the strip in small town America and continued aging the characters; his way of drawing echoed King's style but was tidier and at the same time more richly embellished. Attracted to two of the strip's minor characters, handymen Joel and Rufus, Moores began devoting whole sequences to their bumbling Laurel and Hardy-like escapades (FIGURE 24). Before long, he had made the feature distinctly his own, sustaining its essential ambiance but doing it with his own flair. When Moores died unexpectedly in 1986, his assistant, Jim Scancarelli, took over *Gasoline Alley* (which, by this time, involved both daily strips and the Sunday page); he, too, was able to continue it in much the same fashion as his predecessor, and, like Moores, he added his own touch, making the Alley his just as Moores had done (FIGURES 25-29).

*opposite:* **23.** Bill Perry (about 1920-1990), **Gasoline Alley** (November 24, 1918 - Present ). October 29, 1972. Watercolor, colored pencil, pen and ink on illustration board, 21 × 15 ¼ in. (533 × 387 mm). Collection of Jim Scancarelli. Copyright © 1972 Tribune Media Services. All rights reserved. Reprinted with permission.

By 1972, Walt's children have had children, and Walt is a grandfather. Perry was Frank King's long-time assistant, eventually taking over the Sunday page and continuing it after King's death while Dick Moores conducted the daily strip. Perry hand-colored this page with watercolors and pencil for Jim Scancarelli, the current custodian of *Gasoline Alley.*

# Gasoline Alley

Bill Perry

To MILT, OUR LEADER AND INSPIRATION!
WITH LOVE Dick Moores '78

**24.** Dick Moores (1908-1986), **Gasoline Alley** (November 24, 1918-Present). April 4, 1975. Blue pencil, applied half-tone film, brush, pen and ink on illustration board, 5 × 16³/₈ in. (127 × 416 mm). Milton Caniff Collection, The Ohio State University Cartoon Research Library. Copyright © 1975 Tribune Media Services. All rights reserved. Reprinted with permission.

In defiance of industry expectation, which assumes a strip cannot survive the death of its originator, Moores assumed command of *Gasoline Alley* when Frank King retired in 1960 and not only continued the feature in all its traditional ambiance but improved upon it. Moore's drawing style was in the King tradition but tidier and therefore better suited to the smaller dimension at which strips of the day were being reproduced. Moores dwelt frequently upon the well-intentioned bumbling of two small town handymen, Joel and Rufus. And when Rufus falls in love with the comely Miss Melba, Moores makes sure the course of true love doesn't run too smoothly. (Miss Melba eventually evades the attentions of the other suitor and returns to shy Rufus, her true love—as she is his.)

*Toots and Casper* by Jimmy Murphy (December 17, 1918) was another in the same line. But Sidney Smith's *The Gumps* was of a different order, as we shall see anon. George Herriman's paean to love, *Krazy Kat,* began in the lower portions of a comic strip about family life, *The Family Upstairs* (August 1, 1910, but debuting under the title *The Dingbat Family* on June 20, 1910); Krazy was awarded his own title on October 28, 1913. Animals had populated the Sunday funnies as offshoots of children's literature—Uncle Wiggly (c. 1919) and Peter Rabbit (c. 1920) to name two. But Krazy was different: his message about the enduring quality of love was clearly aimed over the heads of children at adults (FIGURE 14). Most comics always were.

While it is accurate to say that the Sunday supplements were conceived at least in part as entertainment for children, it's worth remembering that the weekly comic magazines, which the supplements imitated, contained political satire and were always directed at adult readers. And daily comic strips, beginning with A. Mutt's wagering compulsion (an adult preoccupation if ever there was one), were clearly intended for adult consumption.

Some cartoonists specialized in a homespun human interest humor, low-key, and usually warmhearted. John T. McCutcheon may have started this trend in 1902 in Chicago with a front-page cartoon depicting a country boy's springtime idling. His work was imitated and elaborated upon by his numerous

( CONTINUED PAGE 50 )

Scancarelli, who had been assisting Moores since 1979, inherited the strip when Moores died unexpectedly in 1986. As the third cartoonist on the feature, Scancarelli maintained the characteristic homespun tone and crisp visuals. Here, his story concerns the two characters Moores spent most of his time on, Joel and Rufus, who, in their habitually maladroit manner, have precipitated the very catastrophe on the bridge from which they rescue the artist.

Scancarelli has proved somewhat more adventurous in his storytelling, sometimes taking the *Gasoline Alley* characters far from the little backwater town that is their accustomed milieu. In this sequence, Scancarelli puts Skeezix into the jungle. Scancarelli has also highlighted such human interest concerns as deafness in the elderly and the naturalization process for the foreign-born.

Scancarelli is particularly pleased with this installment because he engineered a "three panel" strip through ingenious placement of the foreground figures.

28. Jim Scancarelli (Born 1941), **Gasoline Alley** (November 24, 1918 - Present). August 23, 1992. Pasteover, pen and ink on bristol board, 14½ × 20⅝ in. (368 × 524 mm). Mark J. Cohen and Rose Marie McDaniel Collection, The Ohio State University Cartoon Research Library. Copyright © 1992 Tribune Media Services. All rights reserved. Reprinted with permission.

**29.** _____ 1, 1918 - Present). May 20, 1995. Traces of graphite, pasteover, brush, pen and ink on bristol board, 14 1/2 × 20 5/8 in. (368 × 524 mm). Courtesy of the artist. Copyright © 1995 Tribune Media Services. All rights reserved. Reprinted with permission.

On his Sunday pages, Scancarelli frequently waxes nostalgic. Here are two examples that include many of the medium's most popular characters. The May 1995 strip was produced to mark the centennial anniversary of American newspaper comics. Notice that, as Frank King once did, Scancarelli composes the strip as if it were a single bird's-eye view of the mansion that is "the cartoon retirement home," and then imposes a grid of panel borders on the view in order to focus on various aspects of the scene in each of the panels created by the grid.

**30.** Billy DeBeck (1890-1942), **Barney Google** (June 17, 1919- Present, now titled *Snuffy Smith*). August 4, 1931. Traces of graphite, pen and ink on illustration board, 4½ × 17¾ in. (114 × 451 mm). Charles H. Kuhn Collection, The Ohio State Cartoon Research Library. Copyright © 1931. Reprinted with special permission of King Features Syndicate.

Like Bud Fisher's *A. Mutt*, *Barney Google* was initially intended for the sports section of a daily newspaper. Featuring the gag-a-day compulsions of a sports fan in perpetual conflict with his wife about how he spends his time and money, the strip took a sudden turn into day-to-day continuity when Barney acquired a race horse named Spark Plug on July 17, 1922. For the remainder of the decade, readers were held in suspense by DeBeck's skill in building up to the "big race" and then prolonging its outcome. The stereotypical depiction of the African-American trainer-jockey Sunshine was typical of the times. DeBeck achieved a wispy delicacy of shading with cross-hatching that he then scraped with a razor, breaking up the lines to lighten the texture.

contemporaries, Clare Briggs, for instance, and H. T. Webster (who created an American icon for timorousness, Caspar Milquetoast). Beginning in the first decade of the century, both drew daily panel cartoons whose subjects changed from day-to-day, sometimes focusing on the young, sometimes on their parents, the titles suggesting the focus—*When a Feller Needs a Friend, The Days of Real Sport, Ain't It a Grand and Glorious Feelin'?, Timid Soul, The Thrill That Comes Once a Lifetime,* and so on. Thomas A. Dorgan, however—the immortal "Tad" whose specialty was sports—took this kind of humor out of the home sphere and into the workplace and the saloon with his *Indoor Sports* and *Outdoor Sports*. Under the heading *Out Our Way,* J. R. Williams continued the tradition with cartoons about the machine shop and the open range in the West; but he also turned his attention several days a week to home life, depicting the trials and tribulations of children growing up and their effect upon their parents, titling these offerings "Why Mothers Get Gray," "Born Thirty Years Too Soon," and the like (FIGURE 20).

The popularity of the movies inspired several comic strips. Ed Wheelan began the trend with *Midget Movies* (April 8, 1918), which evolved into *Minute Movies* (1921), a strip in which the characters are actors who appear in cinematic productions that constitute the stories of the strip. Chester Gould did one of these, *Fillum Fables* (about 1927) before he concocted one of the world's most famous policemen, Dick Tracy. And E. C. Segar launched his version with *Thimble Theatre* on December 19, 1919. Then on January 17, 1929, Segar introduced the latest in a long line of picturesque secondary characters, but this one took over the strip, and everyone thereafter referred to Segar's strip by the name of this character, Popeye (FIGURE 39).

( CONTINUED PAGE 58 )

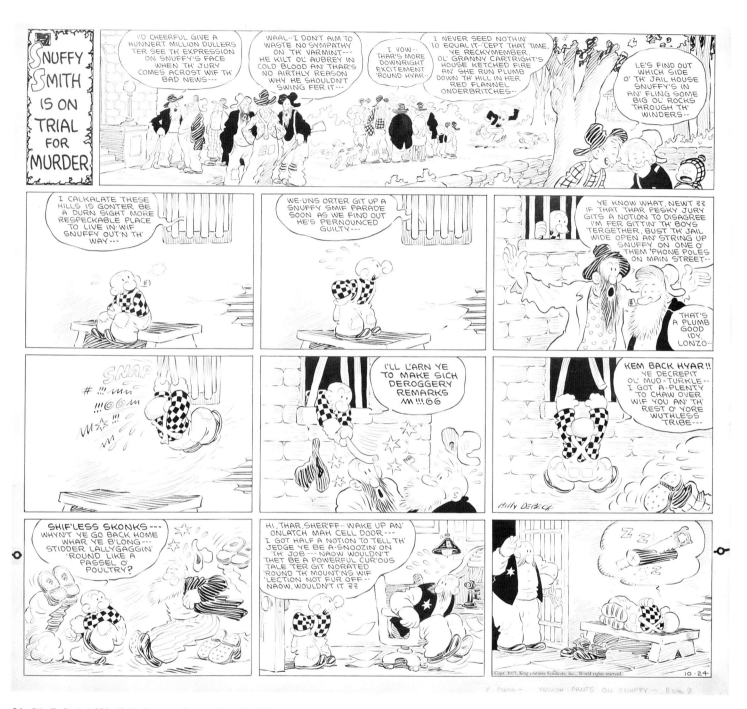

**31.** Billy DeBeck (1890-1942), **Barney Google** (June 17, 1919 - Present, now titled *Snuffy Smith*). October 24, 1937. Traces of graphite, pen and ink on illustration board, 18 1/2 × 20 5/8 in. (473 × 521 mm). Charles H. Kuhn Collection, The Ohio State Cartoon Research Library. Copyright © 1937. Reprinted with special permission of King Features Syndicate.

In the summer of 1934, Barney Google inherits property in the mountains of North Carolina, and when he goes there, he eventually encounters an ornery hillbilly named Snuffy Smith. Snuffy proved so popular a character that within a few years the strip carried his name as well as Barney's; eventually, Barney was displaced altogether. Surprisingly perhaps—considering that the strip was a mere humorous enterprise—DeBeck researched hillbillies thoroughly, amassing a library of reference books on the subject and coining numerous authentic-sounding expressions that subsequently insinuated themselves into popular jargon—"shif'less skonk," "tetched in th' haid," "bodacious idjit," and "time's a-wastin'!" This page displays DeBeck's dextrous penwork, lines that wax thick and wane thin, all from the same flexible pen point.

**32.** Edwina Dumm (1893-1990), **Capt Stubbs and Tippie** (about 1918-1966). September 11, 1933. Pen and ink on illustration board, 6½ x 22½ in. (173 x 573 mm). Edwina Dumm Collection, The Ohio State University Cartoon Research Library. Copyright © 1933 The George Matthew Adams Service, Inc.

One of the longest-lived and truest-to-life comic strips about boyhood was created and sustained through a 48-year run by a woman, Edwina Dumm, who signed her work with her first name alone. Her mature drawing style--relaxed and loose pen-work, open and airy without being sketchy—is ideal for catching in mid-flight the energetic antics of boys and dogs (particularly a wooly-haired mutt) who were constantly on the run, careening headlong down streets and alleys and across vacant lots in passionate pursuit of their latest fancy.

**33.** Gene Byrnes (1889-1974), **Reg'lar Fellers** (about 1916–1949). February 4, 1938. Traces of graphite, brush, pen and ink on single tone Craftint board, 4 x 17 in. (102 x 432 mm). Collection of Mark J. Cohen and Rose Marie McDaniel. Copyright © 1938 George Byrnes.

Another of the most kid-like of the strips about kids is Brynes' strip about Jimmie Dugan, Puddinhead Duffy, and his brother Pinhead (both depicted here) and the rest of the gang in small town America. This sample is atypical: usually, the juvenile characters are in motion, their hyperactive energy suggesting better than anything else their youth. The brown wash here on the Craftint board (now aged) would have reproduced as gray shading.

*opposite:* **34.** Clifford McBride (1901-1951), **Napoleon** (June 6, 1932-1961). October 29, 1933. Traces of graphite, blue pencil, pasteover, pen and ink on illustration board, 21½ x 16½ in. (546 x 413 mm). Collection of Mark J. Cohen and Rose Marie McDaniel. Copyright © 1933 LaFave Newspaper Features.

Distinguished by McBride's energetic penline, *Napoleon* is technically a "dog strip," but the dog, a huge Irish wolfhound, is nearly human in both action and visage. Here, we can see how the layout of a strip—the arrangement and size of the panels—can contribute meaning to the story, in this case, forcing us to a comic comprehension. With the peculiar configuration of Panel 8, McBride ingeniously controls the order in which we gain information while at the same time revealing what is concealed from the boy and the dog: we see the entire scene of the tame circus elephants being watered. The revelation solves some of the mystery that Panel 7 introduces, but we still don't know why the boy and Napoleon are so startled. The position of Panel 8 next forces us to Panel 9 and the explanation: there, we see only what the boy and Napoleon see, the upper part of an elephant, apparently loose in the woods. They flee the vicinity in terror of what they perceive to be an elephant in the wild. On this Sunday strip, the cartoonist has indicated to engravers how to color the strip with notations in light blue (light blue does not photograph in the engraving process).

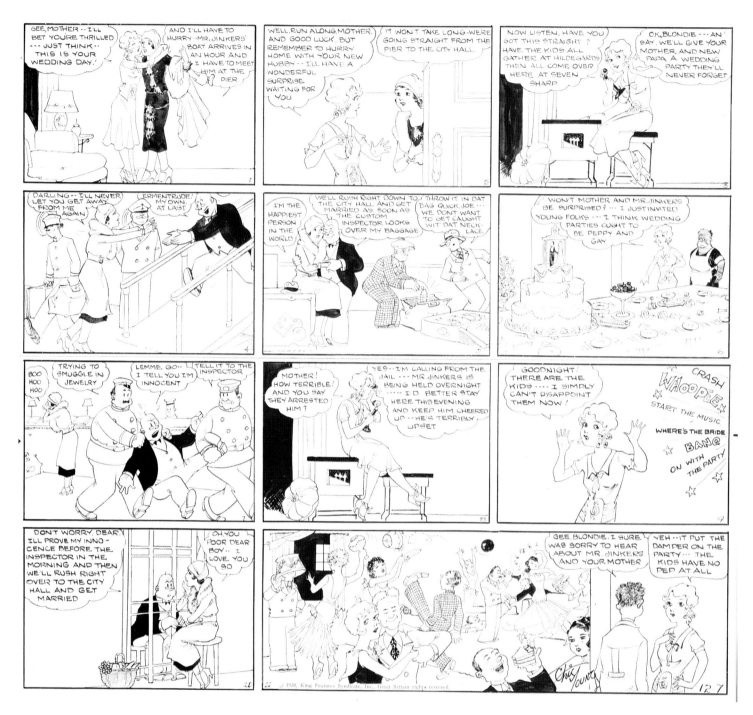

**35.** Chic Young (1901-1973), **Blondie** (September 8, 1930 - Present). December 7, 1930. Traces of graphite, pen and ink on illustration board, 15 × 16½ in. (381 × 416 mm). Collection of Mark J. Cohen and Rose Marie McDaniel. Copyright © 1930. Reprinted with special permission of King Features Syndicate.

Initially, Young's flapper heroine is wholly absorbed in the somewhat frivolous enterprise of attracting male devotees. On Sundays (of which this example is the first), Blondie's mother, who is also single, is engaged in the same activity.

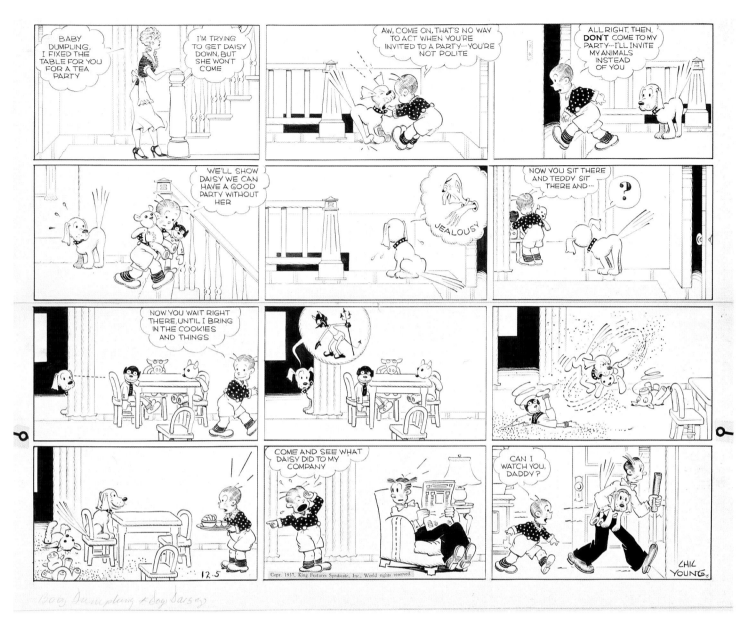

**36.** Chic Young (1901-1973), **Blondie** (September 8, 1930 - Present). December 5, 1937. Traces of graphite, pen and ink on illustration board, 13½ x 17 in. (343 x 432 mm). Philip Sills Collection, The Ohio State University Cartoon Research Library. Copyright © 1937. Reprinted with special permission of King Features Syndicate.

The antics of Blondie and Dagwood in dealing with their new son (not to mention the antics of the offspring) made Blondie one of the most popular strips of the 1930s and established it as a "family strip."

see page 58: **37.** Chic Young, **Blondie**

**37.** Chic Young (1901-1973), **Blondie** (September 8, 1930 - Present). May 4, 1957. Traces of blue pencil, graphite, pen and ink on illustration board, 5 × 17½ in. (128 × 447 mm). Collection of the Cartoon Art Museum, San Francisco. Copyright © 1957. Reprinted with special permission of King Features Syndicate.

Dealing with the everyday concerns of millions of people, *Blondie* had universal appeal and eventually became the most widely published comic strip in history (before being outdistanced by *Peanuts* in the 1960s). By the 1950s, the drawing was being done almost entirely by Young's long-time assistant, Jim Raymond.

With the growing liberation of American women, cartoonists introduced strips aimed at capturing this audience. Cliff Sterrett's *Polly and Her Pals* (December 4, 1912) was among the first of these (FIGURE 18). But while Sterrett found his humor in the contrast between his heroine's attitudes and those of her Victorian parents, Martin Branner explored the life of a working girl in *Winnie Winkle* (September 20, 1920), and Russ Westover did the same in *Tillie the Toiler* (January 3, 1921). And when the flapper emerged in the roaring twenties, she appeared on the comics pages in strips like C. A. Voight's *Betty* (1920), Ernie Bushmiller's *Fritzi Ritz* (1922; which eventually was taken over by Fritzi's niece, Nancy), Edgar Martin's *Boots and Her Buddies* (February 18, 1924), Jefferson Machamer's *Petting Patty* (1928), John Held, Jr.'s *Merely Margy* (1929), and Virginia Huget's *Molly the Manicure Girl* (about 1928), who combined both flapper and working girl (FIGURE 17). In about 1924, Ethel Hays produced a panel cartoon called *Flapper Fanny Says,* which was eventually bequeathed (about 1931) to Gladys Parker, who, later, developed her own feature, *Mopsy* (1939, FIGURE 42).

Another societal preoccupation of the time resulted in the medium's most remarkable mutation. The *Chicago Tribune*'s publisher, Robert McCormick, thought his readers needed help and moral support in learning how to tinker with their automobiles, which, by the mid-teens, were becoming increasingly available to a middle-class public. So he told a staff cartoonist, Frank King, to add a panel about car care to a corner of the weekly page of cartoons and comic sayings that King produced under the title *The Rectangle.* Following the boss's orders, King insinuated a panel of gossip about cars into his weekly mix on November 24, 1918. Called *Gasoline Alley,* the feature ran only on Sundays until the next summer, when, on August 25,

( C O N T I N U E D   P A G E   6 3 )

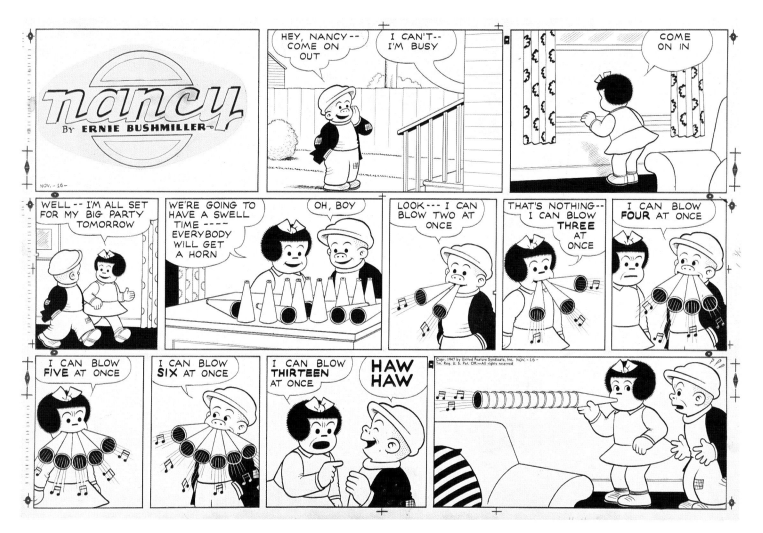

**38.** Ernie Bushmiller (1905-1982), **Nancy** (about 1938-Present). November 16, 1947. Pasteover, pen and ink on illustration board, 15⅛ × 22½ in. (385 × 572). Collection of Mark J. Cohen and Rose Marie McDaniel. Copyright © 1947. NANCY reprinted by permission of United Feature Syndicate, Inc.

Seemingly a "kid strip," *Nancy* is actually a daily exercise in cartooning humor. Bushmiller always blended pictures and words for the comedy; indeed, most of his gags seem to spring from ingenious use of props, and almost none derive at all from the characters (who are, perforce, virtually without personality).

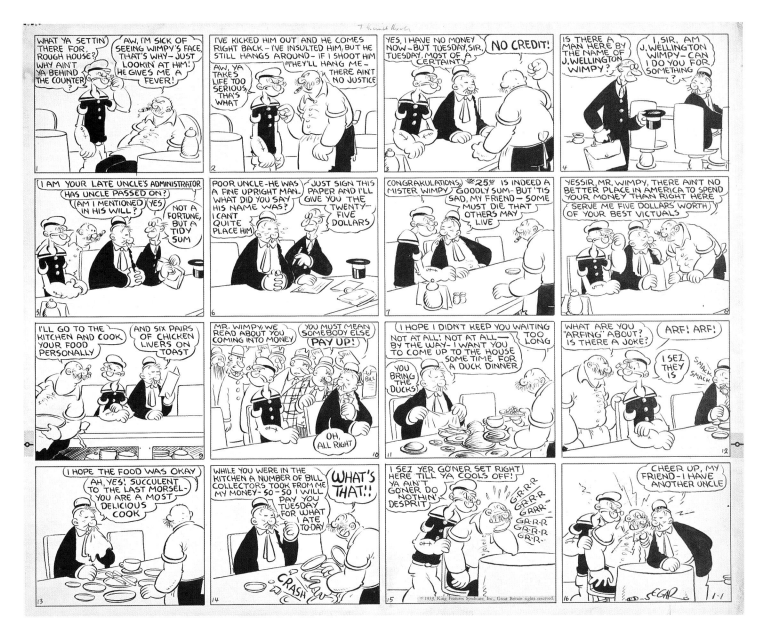

**39.** E. C. Segar (1894-1938), **Thimble Theatre ("Popeye")** (December 19, 1919-Present). January 1, 1933. Pen and ink on illustration board, 16¼ × 20½ in. (413 × 521 mm). Charles H. Kuhn Collection, The Ohio State Cartoon Research Library. Copyright © 1933. Reprinted with special permission of King Features Syndicate.

Segar created two of comic literature's most memorable characters—an invincible fighter as American folk hero and his absolute obverse, an unrepentant louse. Both appear in this strip although Wimpy (the louse and perpetual free-loader) is the principal actor on this Sunday. Visually, Popeye was an inspired construction: his bulging anatomically impossible forearms suggest pugilistic power by bunching all his muscles where they'll be felt the most—right there, behind his knuckles.

**40.** Bill Holman (1903-1987), **Smokey Stover** (March 10, 1935-1971). March 13, 1949. Traces of graphite, pasteover, pen and ink on illustration board, 10 3/4 × 24 in. (273 × 610 mm). Philip Sills Collection, The Ohio State University Cartoon Research Library. Copyright © 1949 Tribune Media Services. All rights reserved. Reprinted with permission.

*Smokey Stover* is a fireman, but Holman's strip is not intended as a reflection of that occupation. An example of how varied the funnies could be, *Smokey Stover* is slapstick in print, full of puns both visual and verbal, and bristling with Holman's mysterious nonsense expressions—"1506 Nix, Nix," "Notary Sojack," and "Foo."

**41.** Vincent T. Hamlin (1900-1993), **Alley Oop** (December 5, 1932 / August 7, 1933 - Present). September 6, 1948. Traces of graphite, blue pencil, pen and ink on illustration board, 5¹/₂ × 20¹/₂ in. (146 × 521 mm). Collection of Laura Shneidman. Copyright © 1948. ALLEY OOP reprinted by permission of Newspaper Enterprise Association, Inc.

Searching for a comic strip theme that would be startlingly different from the futuristic focus of the successful space opera, *Buck Rogers*, Hamlin drew upon his love of geological lore and invented a comic strip set as far in the prehistoric past as *Buck Rogers* was in the future. Beginning with a dinosaur, Hamlin soon concocted a supporting cast—among whom was a cave man named Alley Oop, who quickly took over the strip. *Alley Oop* was picked up in 1933 by the Newspaper Enterprise Association

when the strip's first syndicate collapsed under the weight of the growing Depression. By 1939, Hamlin was growing weary of his hero's antics in the prehistoric kingdom of Moo, and on April 8, he introduced Doctor Wonmug ("one-mug," a play on the German "Ein-stein"), a twentieth century scientist who has invented a time machine. Wonmug employs Oop and his paramour Ooola as field assistants, transporting them to explore the most picturesque eras of the past. (Here, Oop has just returned from Cleopatra's Egypt.) The result, rendered in a delicately hachured style, was a dramatic and sophisticated blend of fact and fantasy, an epic both serious and humorous, the likes of which the comics pages had never seen before. Or since. In short, a masterpiece.

**42.** Gladys Parker (1910-1966), **Mopsy** (about 1939 - 1956). February 26, 1951. Traces of graphite, pen and ink on illustration board, 8¹/₂ × 6 in. (206 × 152 mm). From the Permanent Collection of the International Museum of Cartoon Art, Boca Raton. Copyright © 1951 Associated Newspapers.

A continuation of the flapper girl strip tradition, *Mopsy* focused on men, fashions, money, and jobs. A Sunday strip was added in 1945. Parker, one of the few major female cartoonists of the period, began cartooning in the mid-1920s, but her drawing style was bold and uncluttered compared to the frilly, more decorative work some of her feminine contemporaries produced at that time.

**43.** Gus Arriola (Born 1917). **Gordo** (November 1941- March 2, 1985). About 1941-1942. Traces of graphite, applied half-tone film, pen and ink on illustration board, 6⅛ × 25¾ in. (156 × 654 mm). Collection of Robert C. Harvey. Copyright © 1941. GORDO reprinted by permission of United Feature Syndicate, Inc.

**Evolution of Style I.** At the very beginning, Arriola rendered *Gordo* in the big-foot cartoon style he employed at MGM, where he worked as an animator of Tom and Jerry cartoons. Gordo appears only in the distance here; the characters in the foreground are Juan Pablo and the Poet.

it began to appear every weekday, too. It continued as a single-panel feature, however (with occasional deviations to multiple panels), until about a year later, when it took strip form permanently.

Then in early 1921, the focus of the feature changed dramatically. McCormick's cousin and *Tribune* partner, Joseph Patterson, thought the feature left out women's concerns with all the argot about autos. "Get a baby into the story, fast," he directed the flabbergasted King, who protested that the main character, Walt Wallet, was a bachelor. It was then decided to have Walt find a baby on his doorstep—which he did on Valentine's Day, 1921. With the arrival of the baby Skeezix, the strip developed a strong story line—and with that, day-to-day continuity (FIGURE 21). Walt took weeks trying to settle on a proper name for "Skeezix" (which was merely a slang term like "squirt" or "twirp" or "little shaver"). After running a contest, King decided on Allison—"Alley son." Subsequently, almost accidentally, the strip evolved its most unique feature: its characters aged. To King, this innovative aspect of his strip was simply logical: "You have a one-week-old baby, but he can't stay one week old forever. He had to grow."[12] By logical extension, so did everyone else in the strip. With Skeezix playing a larger and larger role as he grew into boyhood and then manhood, *Gasoline Alley* became, effectively, a family strip (FIGURES 22-29).

Perhaps the most notable of the comic strip inventions of the 1930s was a holdover. Chic Young had displayed a pronounced knack for drawing pretty girls very early in his career. And when he created *Blondie* (September 8, 1930), it was the fourth in a succession of flapper strips he'd launched *(The Affairs of Jane* in 1922, *Beautiful Bab* later the same year, and *Dumb Dora* in 1924), but it wasn't until he put an apron on his heroine that the strip began to climb to its eventual pinnacle as one of the top four or five most widely circulated strips in the world (a position it enjoyed for at least the rest of the century). At first, Blondie was just another dizzy sheba with a flock of beaux left over from the recently departed Jazz Age (FIGURE 35), but when circulation began to slip, Young and syndicate officials decided to let her marry one of her admirers, the scion of a wealthy railroad mogul, who, unfortunately, disapproves of the giddy Blondie. Before the

( C O N T I N U E D   P A G E   6 6 )

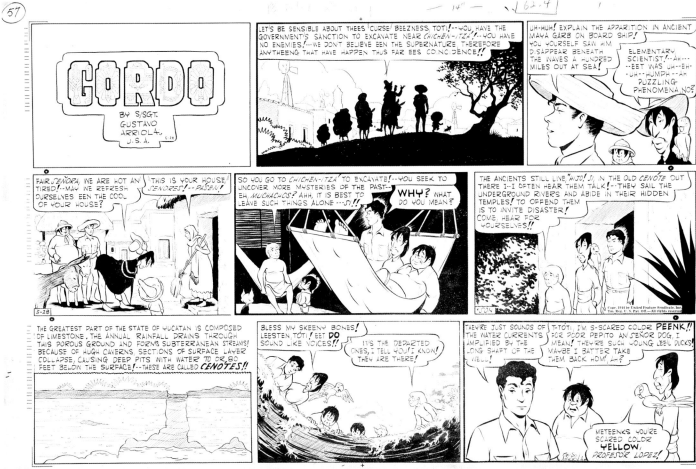

**44.** Gus Arriola (Born 1917), **Gordo** (November 1941-March 2, 1985). May 28, 1944. Traces of blue pencil and graphite, pasteover, white gouache, brush, pen and ink on illustration board, 14 1/2 x 22 1/2 in. (368 x 572 mm). Collection of Mark J. Cohen and Rose Marie McDaniel. Copyright © 1944. GORDO reprinted by permission of United Feature Syndicate, Inc.

**Evolution of Style I.** Upon joining the Army Air Corps in 1942, Arriola discontinued his strip, but when he was stationed in his home town of Los Angeles, producing animated training films, he found time to resume *Gordo* as a Sunday-only feature in May 1943. By this time, his manner of drawing was already evolving into something more realistic than the MGM style with which he had launched the strip: the characters have more human proportions (notice particularly the handsome young man, who would have been impossible in the earlier incarnation of the strip), and wrinkles in clothing are more exactingly depicted.

**45.** Gus Arriola (Born 1917), **Gordo** (November 1941-March 2, 1985). May 2, 1948. Blue pencil, pasteover, pen and ink on illustration board, 15 × 22¹/₂ in. (381 × 572 mm). Collection of Mark J. Cohen and Rose Marie McDaniel. Copyright © 1948. GORDO reprinted by permission of United Feature Syndicate, Inc.

**Evolution of Style I.** Returning to civilian life after the war, Arriola continued to evolve his rendering style. The pictures became more and more realistic (notice the treatment of ears), and, at the same time, the page layout became more decorative, using panels as design elements and accenting the arrangement of these shapes with strategically spotted silhouettes. For a time, Arriola's preliminary sketches were done in blue, as here.

**46.** Gus Arriola (Born 1917), **Gordo** (November 1941-March 2, 1985). September 26, 1963. Traces of blue pencil, brush, pen, and ink on illustration board, 5 1/4 x 19 1/4 in. (101 x 489 mm). Collection of Robert C. Harvey. Copyright © 1963. GORDO reprinted by permission of United Feature Syndicate, Inc.

**Evolution of Style I.** In the mid-1950s, Arriola suddenly—virtually overnight—altered his drawing style dramatically. He simplified. He removed most visual cues intended to evoke a sense of reality (notice the treatment of ears), reduced the depiction of wrinkles in clothing to a few simple lines, adopted a bolder line, and removed all but essential detail from backgrounds. At first, he also treated the backgrounds and props in the strip in a cubist manner, deliberately distorting perspective, for instance. He soon abandoned this maneuver, but the strip remained much more simply drawn than before. He also frequently (but not in this example) deployed a design motif in his daily strips, spotting panels as geometric elements in the design and using silhouettes sometimes extravagantly.

wedding on February 17, 1933, Dagwood Bumstead goes on a twenty-eight-day hunger strike to secure his parents' consent to marry. The ploy worked: the strike revived readership and stimulated sales of the strip—and Dagwood's parents grant him permission to marry Blondie. But they disinherit him.

Dagwood and Blondie were now an ordinary, middle-class married couple, and Dagwood went off to work like husbands all across the land. Their concerns were the concerns of millions of readers, and Young built his daily gags around four of those preoccupations—eating, sleeping, raising a family, and making money—every week offering at least one strip on each topic. In 1934, the Bumsteads had a baby; christened Alexander (after *Flash Gordon* cartoonist Alex Raymond, who had assisted on *Blondie* the preceding year), the boy was called Baby Dumpling, and his arrival sparked another leap in circulation (FIGURE 36). (Tragically, Young's first-born, Wayne, died of jaundice in 1937, in the midst of Baby Dumpling's popularity; a sorrowing Young and his wife took a year-long sabbatical in Europe to recover, while the strip was continued by his assistant, Raymond's brother Jim, who drew the strip until he died in 1981.)

A strip remarkable for its graphic evolution is Gus Arriola's *Gordo*. A pioneer in producing "ethnic" comics, Arriola drew upon his own Mexican heritage in creating a strip about a portly south-of-the-border bean farmer, Gordo, his nephew Pepito, their menagerie (rooster, dog, pig, and more as the years went by), and the farmer's friends (Juan Pablo, the Poet, and Pelon, who ran the local cantina). When the strip started in November 24, 1941, it was rendered in the big-foot style of MGM animated cartoons, upon which Arriola had been working until then (FIGURE 43). But over the years, Arriola dramatically changed his way

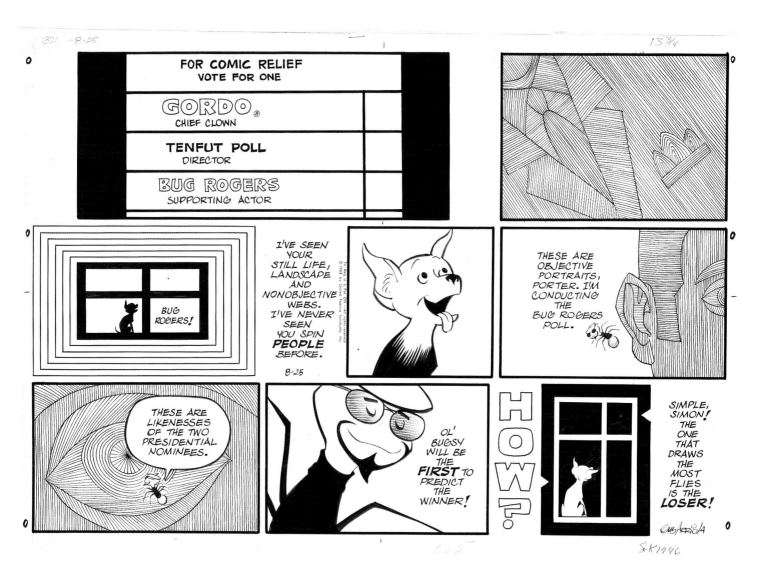

**47.** Gus Arriola (Born 1917), **Gordo** (November 1941- March 2, 1985). August 25, 1968. Blue pencil, brush, pen and ink on bristol board, 15¼ x 22⅝ in. (387 x 574 mm). Collection of Mark J. Cohen and Rose Marie McDaniel. Copyright © 1968. GORDO reprinted by permission of United Feature Syndicate, Inc.

**Evolution of Style I.** In the 1950s, Arriola's Sunday pages became fiestas of color and design, and by the next decade, a spider named Bug Rogers was frequently the featured player, spinning his webs into intricate shapes and patterns, all littered with puns of the very worst (which is to say, the best) sort. The designs in the non-web panels here are evocative of the Dutch abstract artist Piet Mondrian.

"ALVIN! YOU SHAVED!"

**48.** Marty Links (Born about 1924), **Emmy Lou** (about 1951-1979). December 14, 1960. Traces of graphite, brush, pen and ink on illustration board, 8½ × 7 in. (216 × 178 mm). Collection of the Cartoon Art Museum, San Francisco. Copyright ©1960. EMMY LOU reprinted by permission of United Feature Syndicate, Inc.

The "kid strips" of the century's first quarter were replaced in the 1940s by features about the newest social phenomenon, teenagers—or, as the females of the breed were called then, "bobby soxers." When *Emmy Lou* began in 1944 it was called *Bobby Sox*, but the title spotlight shifted to one of the principal players in 1951. At the time Links launched the feature, she was in a pretty exclusive club: syndicated women cartoonists numbered less than half-a-dozen.

of drawing, producing eventually the decorative masterpiece of the comics page, the envy of his colleagues (FIGURE 47). He frequently made the strip educational, informing his readers about the culture of Mexico, but he was continually criticized for the stereotypical lingo his characters spoke. Gradually, Arriola softened the dialect until it disappeared altogether (FIGURE 46). "I realized," he said, "that I was depicting a people—my people. And Gordo was the only strip here that's actually located outside this country. So I started to use jokes other than ethnic." Gordo became a tour bus driver and rather sophisticated, and when the strip ceased March 2, 1985, Arriola gave his forty-three-year saga an ending, marrying Gordo to his long-time housekeeper, Tehuana Mama.

In all of these enterprises, words are yoked to pictures as a matter of course. In the best examples of the art, however, the verbal and the visual are blended, neither word nor picture making complete sense without the other, and both together conveying a meaning neither can achieve alone. Not all comic strips strike a perfect visual-verbal balance in every installment, but the principle suggests a measure by which comic strip artistry can be evaluated. Such a criterion is scarcely the only one or the only valid one. Perhaps its more significant usefulness is that it provides a method, a procedure—a way of coming at an understanding and appreciation of comic art. I think of it as a way of "tuning up," of getting our sensibilities attuned to the special rhythms of an art form that is simultaneously both visual and verbal. ●

# Continuity: Soap Opera and Adventure and the Advent of the Illustrator

## MOVEMENT 3

THE FORM OF THE COMIC STRIP was securely in place by the time *Mutt and Jeff* was achieving national notoriety in the century's second decade. And the form would not change significantly. But the way cartoonists deployed this form would continue to evolve. To backtrack a bit for the sake of our third movement, the first step in that evolution was taken in the early 1920s in the pages of the *Chicago Tribune,* and that step was taken not by a cartoonist but by an editor.

Joseph Medill Patterson did not exactly invent the continuity strip—a comic strip that told a story that continued from day to day. But the legendary "Captain" Patterson certainly midwifed at its birth and nursed it into healthy infancy.

Patterson's inspiration for a continuity strip may have arisen from his early experience while in charge of the Sunday *Chicago Tribune.* Noting readers' favorable response to a directory he began that listed current attractions at Chicago movie theaters, Patterson soon hit upon a way of exploiting the public's fascination with the "flickers." Making a deal with William Selig, the producer of one of the first movie serials, *The Adventures of Kathlyn,* Patterson began on January 4, 1914, to publish a written version of each week's episode, the week before the next film installment appeared. Readers could win prizes by guessing the solutions to mysteries in each week's printed version. *The Adventures of Kathlyn* ran for twenty-six weeks, and each week the *Tribune's* circulation increased. The lesson was not lost on the canny Captain. The basic element in the project had been continuation: the reader (the newspaper buyer) had to buy the next Sunday *Chicago Tribune* to see how the stories came out. When Patterson turned his attention to the funnies, that idea was doubtless not far below the surface in his thinking.

Comic strips that told continuing stories had been around long before Captain Patterson took an interest in the idea. McCay's *Little Nemo in Slumberland* had continued its narrative from Sunday to Sunday

(CONTINUED PAGE 74)

**49.** Sidney Smith (1877-1935), **The Gumps** (February 12, 1917- October 17, 1959). May 23, 1921. Traces of graphite, pasteovers, pen and ink on illustration board, 5 5/8 x 20 5/8 in. (143 x 524 mm). Charles H. Kuhn Collection, The Ohio State University Cartoon Research Library.

In its preoccupation with the domestic doings of Andy and Min Gump and their relatives, *The Gumps* was the first "soap opera" strip (before, even, the coining of the term). It was also the first seriously intended continuity strip.

**50.** Roy Crane (1901-1977), **Wash Tubbs** (April 21, 1924-about 1988). May 16, 1933. Traces of blue pencil, pen and ink on illustration board, 5 1/2 x 24 1/2 in. (140 x 622 mm). Collection of Robert Stolzer. Copyright © 1933. WASH TUBBS reprinted by permission of Newspaper Enterprise Association, Inc.

Drawing in a traditional (or "big foot") cartoony manner for most human figures, Crane created an aura of realism with his more illustrative rendition of props and locales. He also experimented with cross-hatching, crayon, and other shading techniques to give his settings a more realistic appearance.

**51.** Roy Crane (1901-1977), **Wash Tubbs** (April 21, 1924-about 1988). February 6, 1938. Sunday half-page. Traces of graphite, blue pencil, brush, pen and ink on illustration board, 12 ½ × 20 ½ in. (318 × 521 mm). Collection of Robert Stolzer. Copyright © 1938. WASH TUBBS reprinted by permission of Newspaper Enterprise Association, Inc.

Captain Easy was so popular a character that he took over the Sunday page in 1933. In this half-page from 1938, Crane demonstrates his imaginative approach to page layout, varying the size and shape of panels in order to make better use of the visuals in creating the mood and the ambiance of the locale. Although his linework was simple, it was precise, and in its precision, it was perfection. Wash's trousers in the central panel on the second tier of this layout could scarcely have been depicted more simply—or more accurately.

*see page 70:* **49.** Sidney Smith, **The Gumps**

**52.** Roy Crane (1901-1977), **Wash Tubbs** (April 21, 1924 - about 1988). February 3, 1940. Brush, pen and ink on double tone Craftint board, 4 ½ × 20 ½ in. (114 × 521 mm). Collection of Frank Pauer. Copyright © 1940. WASH TUBBS reprinted by permission of Newspaper Enterprise Association, Inc.

By the late 1930s, Crane had abandoned his various experiments with shading (crayon, pencil, cross-hatching) in favor of a chemically-treated drawing paper called Craftint, which, when treated with a brushed-on liquid, produced two tones of gray and a nearly photographic appearance.

from the very beginning. And Fisher had capitalized on the daily appearance of *A. Mutt,* postponing until the next day the announcement of the outcome of Mutt's daily wager. Moreover, in 1906 C. W. Kahles introduced *Hairbreadth Harry,* a Sunday strip that burlesqued adventure stories, ending each week's installment with a hilarious cliffhanger that would not be resolved until the next week. And Harry Hershfield did the same sort of thing in *Desperate Desmond* (1910) and *Dauntless Durham* (1913). The film-inspired strips like *Minute Movies* and *Thimble Theatre* told continuing stories, also, albeit infected with an element of self-deprecating mockery.

But if Patterson didn't invent the continuity strip, he and Sidney Smith refined the idea in a way that opened the door to the future, to continuity strips of exotic serious adventure: *The Gumps* made suspense the driving mechanism of the continuity strip.

When Patterson began thinking about a new comic strip in early 1917, he envisioned something considerably more in touch with everyday reality than the mock heroicism in the strips done by Kahles and Hershfield. The Captain wanted social realism like that found in the novels of Theodore Dreiser (and in Patterson's own fiction, like his 1908 novel *A Little Brother of the Rich,* which he produced before assuming the editorial throne at the *Tribune).* He directed Smith, a staff cartoonist then producing a strip about goats

*opposite:* **53.** Hal Forrest (about 1892 - 1959), **Tailspin Tommy** (July 19, 1928 - about 1942). June 19, 1931. Watercolor, pen and ink on illustration board, 28 ½ × 22 in. (730 × 559). Collection of Mark J. Cohen and Rose Marie McDaniel.

Although Forrest's art is enhanced here considerably by the addition of color, it remains somewhat primitive, the pen technique so rudimentary and monotonous as to mask whatever successes he might have achieved in his pencil renditions of anatomy and physiognomy.

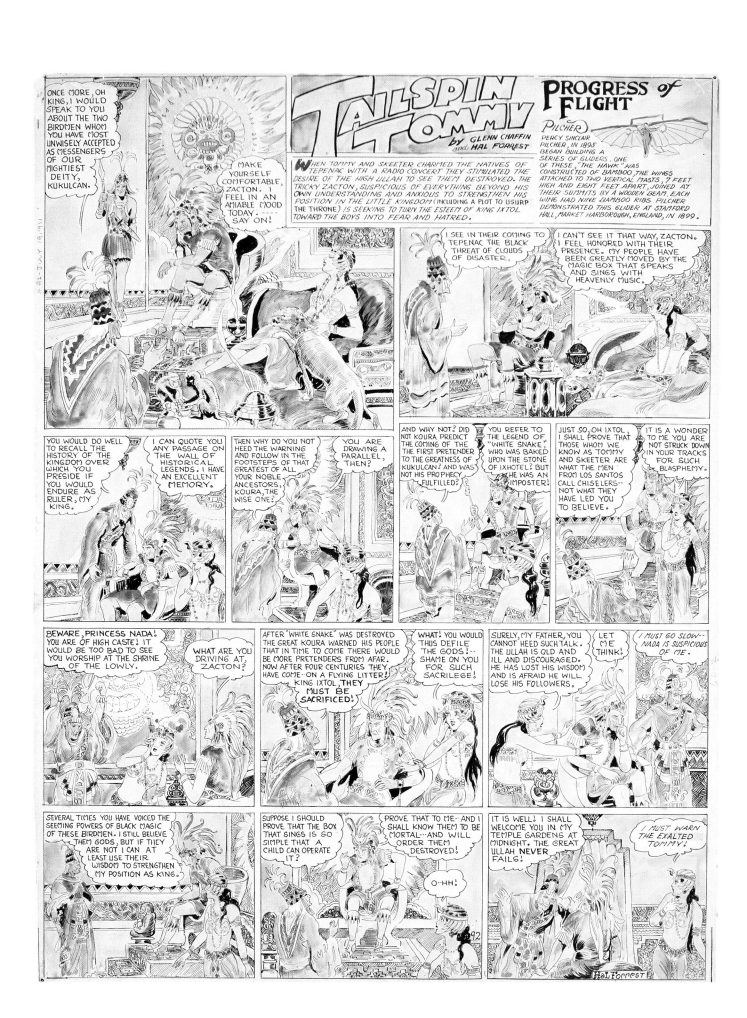

**54.** Lyman Young (1893-1984), **Tim Tyler's Luck** (August 13, 1928 - July 31, 1972). April 25, 1933. Traces of blue pencil, brush, pen and ink on illustration board, 5 3/8 × 24 7/8 in. (137 × 638 mm). Collection of the Cartoon Art Museum, San Francisco. Copyright © 1933. Reprinted with special permission of King Features Syndicate.

Starting as a Horatio Alger epic, *Tim Tyler's Luck* turned to aviation and then to general adventure. Young, whose style was cartoony rather than illustrative, employed a succession of ghost artists, who drew more realistically than he, to illuminate the adventures. In 1933, one of those who worked with Young was Alex Raymond, whose skill vastly improved the look of the strip.

called *Old Doc Yak,* to devise a strip that could achieve both comedy and catastrophe by focusing on an average, lower-middle-class family. Patterson named the family, employing a slightly derisive term that he and his sister Cissie had applied as children to loudmouthed adults. In Andy Gump's case, the name was a self-fulfilling prophecy (FIGURE 49).

Although Smith offered a slight thread of continuity in the strip from the beginning on February 12, 1917 (the Gumps move into the house Doc Yak rented, displacing the goat—and his strip—from the paper), he didn't hit his stride with suspenseful action until 1921, when Andy's millionaire relation, Uncle Bim, fell into the clutches of the Widow Zander. A gold-digging damsel, her marital intentions for Bim threaten Andy's hopes of inheriting his uncle's fortune (a preoccupation that animates many of Andy's soliloquies over the years).

Once Smith warmed to his task, he soaped his stories with every sudsy bubble of melodrama he could squeeze out of his pen. He was able to prolong the Widow Zander affair for most of 1921 and into the next year, and that year, Andy Gump ran for Congress. The blowhard was in his natural element. By this time, people were asking newsdealers for "the Gump paper," not the *Chicago Tribune.* Reading the strip every day had become a habit, if not an addiction, among its readers. Suspenseful continuity as a device for building

(CONTINUED PAGE 81)

*opposite:* **55.** Harold R. Foster (1892-1982), **Tarzan** (March 15, 1931- Present) (Foster's tenure, September 17, 1931-May 2, 1937). December 2, 1934. Traces of graphite, pasteover, red ink, brush, pen and ink on illustration board, 26 3/8 × 19 5/8 in. (670 × 498 mm). Collection of Jack Gilbert. Copyright © 1934. TARZAN reprinted by permission of United Feature Syndicate, Inc.

The first illustrator of top rank to work in comics, Foster demonstrated, during his stint on the Sunday Tarzan pages, that high quality realistic artwork could heighten the drama of adventure storytelling strips by making the characters and the locales seem real.

# Tarzan

## by EDGAR RICE BURROUGHS

**SACRIFICE**

WHILE THE ISLAND SAVAGES FLED IN TERROR, BELIEVING THE BEASTS WERE DEMONS CONJURED UP BY TARZAN, A LION CHARGED AT PRINCESS MIHRAMA.

THE JUNGLE LORD, FIGHTING HIS WAY OUT OF THE ENGULFING WAVE OF FRANTIC WAIORIS, HEARD THE MAIDEN'S CRY AND SAW HER JEOPARDY.

HE CLIMBED ABOVE THE HUMAN TIDE AND SKIPPED ALONG THE SHOULDERS OF THE CLOSE-PRESSED HORDE AS HE MIGHT RACE THROUGH SWAYING TREES.

AGAIN ON SOLID EARTH, HE RAN LIKE THE WIND. A WILD CRY TOLD HIM THAT BOHGDU, HIS FAITHFUL APE HAD ESCAPED TOO, AND TARZAN CALLED TO HIM.

TARZAN ARRIVED AS THE LION LEAPED AT THE GIRL. HE FLUNG HIS WEIGHT AGAINST THE BEAST, AND PLUNGED HIS KNIFE THROUGH THE TAWNY HIDE.

AS THE LION LAY DEAD, TARZAN COMMANDED THE APE TO BEAR THE PRINCESS AWAY TO SOME HIGH TREE AND DEPOSIT HER THERE FOR SAFETY.

WHEN BOHGDU RETURNED, THE TWO DRAGGED THEIR FRIENDS FREE FROM THE FRENZIED SAVAGES, AND TARZAN ORDERED THEM SOUTHWARD TO THE SHORE.

THEN THE APE-MAN RETRIEVED THE MAIDEN AND HURRIED THROUGH THE TREETOPS TO THE WATERSIDE RENDEZVOUS.

FAR EASTWARD ALONG THE BEACH, THE PARTY CAME UPON A SMALL BOAT, GUARDED BY TWO WARRIORS.

TARZAN AND BOHGDU SPRANG UPON THEM, DISARMED THEM, AND HURLED THEM INTO THE SEA.

TWO MUST REMAIN ON THE ISLAND TO BRAVE THE WRATH OF DESTER MOLU! "THE APE SHALL STAY," SAID TARZAN CALMLY; "AND I STAY WITH HIM!"

BUT WHEN THE FUGITIVES CAME TO EMBARK, THEY FOUND THAT THE TINY CRAFT COULD NOT CONTAIN THEM ALL!

**NEXT WEEK: *THE GAGE OF BATTLE***

**56.** Burne Hogarth (1911-1996), **Tarzan** (March 15, 1931-Present) (Hogarth's tenure, May 9, 1937-mid-August 1950, with a break around 1945-1947). August 6, 1950. Traces of graphite, red ink, pasteover, brush, pen and ink on illustration board, 18½ × 27½ in. (470 × 699 mm). Collection of Jack Gilbert. Copyright © 1950. TARZAN is reprinted by permission of United Feature Syndicate, Inc.

Foster's successor on *Tarzan*, Hogarth made his mark through the sheer flamboyance of his style: the protagonist's physique seems flayed of the first layers of skin to reveal the underlying musculature, the poses are highly dramatic albeit wholly unlikely, and the scenery itself seems alive with menace. Hogarth's technique was markedly different from Foster's. The realism of Foster's manner convinces us that even impossible feats are possible: Foster shows how they would be done by a real person if they could be done. Hogarth, on the other hand, persuades us to believe in the achievements of his character through the visual rhetoric of his rendering: the dynamic of Tarzan's anatomy convinces us that his character is capable of whatever superhuman effort is necessary to accomplish the impossible. Compare the foreshortened Tarzan running in Foster's fourth panel with Hogarth's third panel: identical poses, but Hogarth's Tarzan is pitched forward at an impossible angle; Foster's is not. Still, both versions are convincing: Foster's through realism alone; Hogarth's through the energetic ballet of his character's pose. The red lines in some of the panels here are guides to the engravers, indicating how the color in various places should be applied (the red lines are filtered out in the plate-making process). In some of the instances at hand, the color will simply not be applied, creating a white "highlight" on a bush or leaf or tree trunk; in other instances, the background color for a particular panel will not run up to the ruled border but will stop where the red line is.

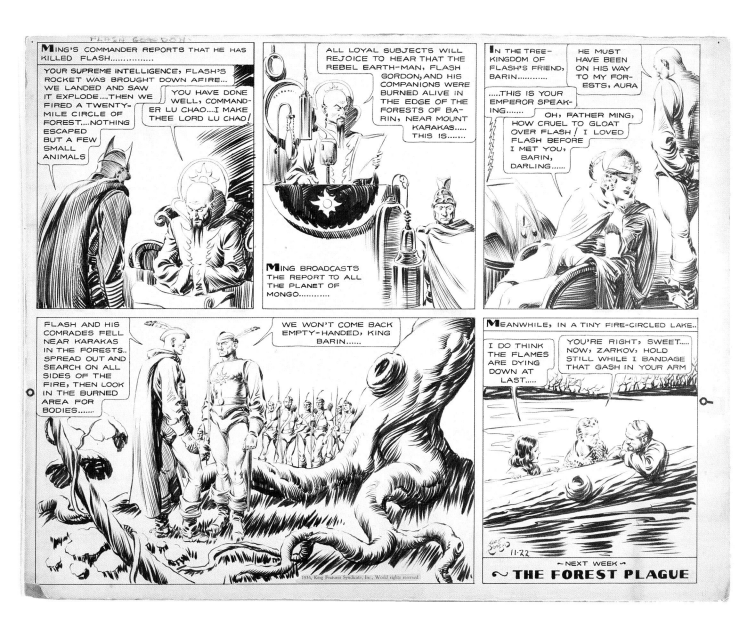

**57.** Alex Raymond (1909-1956), **Flash Gordon** (January 7, 1934 - Present) (Raymond's tenure, January 7, 1934 - April 30, 1944). November 22, 1936. Brush, pen and ink on illustration board, 15½ x 19⅞ in. (400 x 505 mm). Charles H. Kuhn Collection, The Ohio State University Cartoon Research Library. Copyright © 1936. Reprinted with special permission of King Features Syndicate.

*Flash Gordon* tells how the planet Mongo is saved by the interloper Flash and his friends Dale Arden and Doctor Hans Zarkov from the cruel ministrations of the Emperor, Ming the Merciless. Written by Don Moore, the story, while thoroughly competent and often ingenious, was not particularly inspired. But Raymond's drawings were. His exquisite renderings—his fantastic locales, gorgeously sexy women, and ruggedly handsome men—gave the space opera so persuasive an illusion of reality that *Flash Gordon* became a part of the American cultural heritage. Influenced at an early stage by illustrator Matt Clark, Raymond resorted enthusiastically to dry brush to model and embellish his pictures.

**58.** Alex Raymond (1909-1956), **Flash Gordon** (January 7, 1934 - Present) (Raymond's tenure, January 7, 1934 - April 30, 1944). November 12, 1939. Traces of graphite, red ink, brush, pen and ink on illustration board, 19½ x 24 in. (495 x 610 mm). Collection of Ethan Roberts. Copyright © 1939. Reprinted with special permission of King Features Syndicate.

By 1939, Raymond was working meticulously with a pen as well as a brush. The characters are wearing special transparent underwater outer garb for this adventure. Raymond's achievement inspired a generation of cartoonists, all of whom sought to enhance the drama of their adventure strips with the authenticity of the illustrative manner.

**59.** Alex Raymond (1909-1956), **Rip Kirby** (March 4, 1946 - Present). July 4, 1947. Traces of blue pencil, brush, pen and ink on illustration board, 5 1/2 × 18 5/8 in. (140 × 473 mm). From the Permanent Collection of the International Museum of Cartoon Art, Boca Raton. Copyright © 1947. Reprinted with special permission of King Features Syndicate.

Raymond left *Flash Gordon* in the winter of 1944 to join the Marine Corps. When he returned to civilian life, he launched a new daily-only comic strip, *Rip Kirby*, destined to be his fourth successful effort, an unprecedented achievement for a cartoonist at that time. Kirby, a detective, was also unprecedented: although an ex-Marine, he was decidedly urbane, wearing glasses (which made him unmistakably an intellectual), dressing fashionably, moving in the best social circles, employing a butler, and having a fashion model as a girlfriend. Assisted in scripting chores by writers and editors in the King Features bullpen, Raymond developed a distinctive illustrative technique that set the strip apart from his earlier work by deploying solid blacks and bold brushstrokes in dramatic contrast to the fine-line penwork, another stylistic triumph. Raymond sometimes stumbled in storytelling however: the secondary characters in the last two panels shown here look too much alike. At first glance, the reader might assume them to be the same person. Reversing the lettering on the door is a last-minute nudge at helping the reader decipher the situation correctly.

a successful comic strip was established. The next step was to make that suspense life-threatening: the serious adventure strip was just on the horizon.

Strips that told a continuing story from day to day were inherently suspenseful: the serial format could not help but create a daily cliff-hanger. And it did not take cartoonists long to realize that a cliff-hanger gained in emotional power if the characters left dangling were in danger of losing life or limb. Life-threatening danger in turn meant life-threatening action—in short, adventure, action packed and danger-laden. And the adventure strip was made-to-order for service in the circulation battles of daily newspapers. What better inducement could an editor contrive for getting the public to buy his paper every day than to promise readers, each day, the resolution of yesterday's comic strip cliff-hanger?

Several comic strips took tentative steps in the adventure arena before the genre was successfully established. Harold Gray set the pace for awhile with *Little Orphan Annie,* which, beginning August 5, 1924, inspired numerous forays with unfortunate, albeit spunky, foundlings. Among them were such pioneering efforts as *Phil Hardy* (November 1925) drawn by George Storm and written by Jay Jerome Williams, and (taking the place of *Hardy,* which had expired in the fall of 1926) *Bobby Thatcher* (May 1927), also drawn by Storm. But these urchin epics were often more soap opera than adventure: their stock in trade was emotional travail, not physical action. Moreover, they were all grimly serious: what adventure there was

(CONTINUED PAGE 85)

AND ANOTHER PERIL ASSAILS THEM; UNDER THE TERRIBLE, CONSTANT STRAIN SEAMS ARE BEGINNING TO OPEN IN THE VESSEL'S HULL!

THEN THE WILD STORM GOES LEAPING BY TO BATTER MARINERS ON OTHER SEAS. A COAST LOOMS UP BEFORE THEM AND THERE IS GREAT JOY, FOR THEIR SHIP IS LEAKING BADLY AND DRINKING WATER DESPERATELY LOW.

A SHELTERED BAY OPENS BEFORE THEM AND THEY COME GLIDING IN FROM THE TURBULENT SEA TO FIND REST, WATER AND A SANDY BEACH ON WHICH TO CAREEN THEIR SHIP.

ALETA STEPS ASHORE AND HEADS STRAIGHT FOR A SPARKLING BROOK.....AFTER ALL, GO JUST SO LONG WITHOUT A BATH!

FAR OUT ON THE BAY TWO HEADS CAN BE SEEN BOBBING ON THE WAVES, ONE SHINY BLACK, THE OTHER GOLDEN IN THE SUNLIGHT.

NEXT WEEK:— Ireland!

**60.** Harold R. Foster (1892-1982), **Prince Valiant** (February 13, 1937-Present). April 11, 1948 (bottom ⅔ of the page). Traces of blue pencil and graphite, red ink, brush, pen and ink on illustration board, 22 ½ × 24 ¼ in. (572 × 616 mm). Milton Caniff Collection, The Ohio State University Cartoon Research Library. Copyright ©1948. Reprinted with special permission of King Features Syndicate.

Foster's superb ability as an illustrator gave his saga of a knight in the days of King Arthur a palpable reality. Foster researched his medieval milieu thoroughly and gave painstaking attention to every illustrative detail, whether in rendering rocky shorelines or Viking mariners.

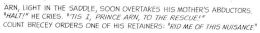

**61.** Harold R. Foster (1892-1982), **Prince Valiant** (February 13, 1937- Present). March 15, 1964. Traces of blue pencil and graphite, pasteover, red ink, pen and ink on illustration board, 34 x 22 ³/₄ in. (864 x 578 mm). Collection of Ethan Roberts. Copyright ©1964. Reprinted with special permission of King Features Syndicate.

Foster was equally adept at depicting action (caught here in the fourth panel with photographic accuracy just after Val strikes a blow) and the facial expressions of his characters. Aleta (the "small blonde" who is wife to Valiant and mother to Arn) has been kidnapped but is scarcely a submissive captive: in the previous week's installment, she attacked one of her captors and left him behind; in the first panel here, Val and Arn come upon her hapless victim and appropriate some of his equipage. Then, through a ruse, father and son begin whittling down the number of their foe, and Aleta holds firm, as always.

**62.** Chester Gould (1900 - 1985), **Dick Tracy** (October 4, 1931- Present). May 19, 1944. Traces of graphite, pen and ink on illustration board, 6 × 19 ⁷/₈ in. (152 × 505 mm). Collection of Matt Masterson. Copyright © 1944 Tribune Media Services. All rights reserved. Reprinted with permission.

   Although not rendered in the illustrative manner emerging in the 1930s as the fashion for storytelling strips, *Dick Tracy* captured the attention of readers immediately with its stark and often bloody portrayal of the battle between cops and crooks. With his somewhat cartoony style, Gould could moralize in his strips by using grotesque caricatures of evil for his villains. He could also find humor in his milieu—here, with ham actor Vitamin Flintheart, who was as addicted to pills as his look-alike John Barrymore was to alcohol.

**63.** Chester Gould (1900-1985), **Dick Tracy** (October 4, 1931- Present). August 21, 1953. Traces of graphite, pen and ink on illustration board, 5 × 16 ¹/₂ in. (127 × 419 mm). From the Permanent Collection of the International Museum of Cartoon Art, Boca Raton. Copyright © 1953 Tribune Media Services. All rights reserved. Reprinted with permission.

   Dick Tracy achieved the illusion of reality with the black-and-white diagrammatic accuracy of Gould's drawings of locales and equipage, and by employing authentic police procedures in tracking criminals and fighting crime. Here, we see another brace of Gould's comedy characters, the farmer B.O. Plenty and his wife, Gravel Gertie; in the first panels, Tracy's former side-kick, Pat Patton, who has become the chief of police, and Tracy's new partner, Sam Catchem.

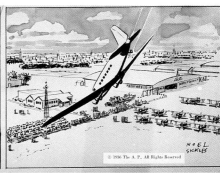

**64.** Noel Sickles (1910-1982), **Scorchy Smith** (about 1930-1961) (Sickles' term, about 1934-1936). July18, 1936. Brush, pen and ink on Craftint board, 4 1/2 × 21 in. (117 × 533 mm). Collection of Ethan Roberts. Copyright © 1936 The Associated Press. All rights reserved.

Sickles, seeking a way to produce quality illustration within the time limits imposed by weekly deadlines for daily strips, hit upon a way of doing convincingly realistic pictures by using solid black shadows to create a visual impression of images rather than by drawing every detail—every wrinkle and fold in clothing, every rivet on an airplane's wing. Milton Caniff, with whom Sickles shared a studio in the early days of Caniff's work on *Terry and the Pirates*, learned Sickles' technique and made it famous—and widely imitated. By the summer of 1936 when this example was published, Sickles had introduced yet another refinement on his method: he modulated the stark chiaroscuro black-and-white contrast of his earlier experiment by using a Craftint process to create a medium gray tone, enhancing the photographic impression of his treatment. What appears here to be a brown wash is actually all that remains of the Craftint shading, which, with age, has deteriorated, the original dot pattern fading away entirely.

didn't look like much fun for the adventurers. And somehow, we like to think, adventuring ought to be fun: adventuring promises excitement, and excitement is an aspect of fun. This vital aspect of the adventure strip genre was virtually invented by Roy Crane.

Crane's historic achievement was to set the pace for adventure strips in the "adventurous decade" of the thirties by showing the way in the twenties. Many of those who drew the earliest adventure strips were inspired and influenced by his work. We recognize the milestones in the history of the comics that mark the accomplishments of such creators as Chester Gould, Alex Raymond, Hal Foster, Ham Fisher, and Milton Caniff. But we forget sometimes that Crane preceded them all onto the stage they later filled with their presence. And most of them, as they felt their way in developing adventure storytelling skills, looked to Crane for hints about how to do it.

Crane's magnum opus, *Washington Tubbs II* (or, simply, *Wash Tubbs)* began April 21, 1924. But not as an adventure strip. It was, rather, a gag-a-day strip about a diminutive curly headed, bespectacled young clerk in a grocery store, a sort of brash version of Harold Lloyd, with soaring ambitions for amorous conquest and financial gain. Soon Crane, bored with thinking up jokes for his pint-sized protagonist, found himself dreaming of his younger days bumming across the country in box cars or shipping out to sea on a freighter. Since he couldn't resume this carefree life himself, he sent Wash on a treasure hunt to the South Pacific, the first of several such adventures.

*Wash Tubbs* remained a thoroughly humorous strip: with its ebullient hero, reaching always to fantastic heights quite above his stature, it could scarcely be anything else. But by 1927, deliberate daily gags had

( CONTINUED PAGE 91 )

**65.** Milton Caniff (1907-1988), **Terry and the Pirates** (October 22, 1934-February 23, 1973) (Caniff's tenure, October 22, 1934-December 29, 1946). November 10, 1934. Blue pencil, brush, pen and ink on illustration board, 6 x 21 in. (152 x 533 mm). Private collection, Seattle. Copyright © 1934 Tribune Media Services. All rights reserved. Reprinted with permission.

**66.** Milton Caniff (1907-1988), **Terry and the Pirates** (October 22, 1934-February 23, 1973) (Caniff's tenure, October 22, 1934-December 29, 1946). December 17, 1945. Traces of graphite, brush and ink on illustration board, 7 3/8 x 21 5/8 in. (187 x 549 mm). Private collection, Seattle. Copyright © 1945 Tribune Media Services. All rights reserved. Reprinted with permission.

      **Evolution of Style II.** Caniff's impact on the visual aspects of the art form is dramatically demonstrated by contrasting a strip from the first month of *Terry and the Pirates* (Figure 65) with one from Caniff's last year on the strip. Simply stated, the artist shifted from pen to brush and cloaked his drawings in shadow; but this simple maneuver achieved a stunning illusion of reality. The chiaroscuro technique that Caniff perfected was widely imitated by those cartoonists doing adventure strips who were not aping Raymond or Foster. Note also the dramatic storytelling effect of changing the point of view in the last panel of the 1934 strip and, in the later example, the power of authentic lingo in creating narrative tension.

**67.** Milton Caniff (1907-1988), **Terry and the Pirates** (October 22, 1934-February 23, 1973) (Caniff's tenure, October 22, 1934 - December 29, 1946). August 16, 1936. Panel. Traces of blue pencil, brush, pen and ink on illustration board, 6 1/4 × 6 1/8 in. (159 × 156 mm). Milton Caniff Collection, The Ohio State University Cartoon Research Library. Copyright © 1936 Tribune Media Services. All rights reserved. Reprinted with permission.

**Evolution of Style II.** The essence of the chiaroscuro technique is to indicate shapes with shadows rather than with lines. In Caniff's earliest deployment of this technique (as in this panel), figures and objects are outlined in pen, and then the side away from a light source is filled in with solid black to create the "shadow" cast by the light. The light is shining from the left in this panel, and the figure in the foreground is entirely in the shadow of the building against which the character reposes (creating a dramatic frame for the principal characters in mid-panel). Clearly, this technique saved a great deal of time and effort; it also heightened the black-and-white contrast in the artwork, creating spectacular pictures that leaped off the pages at the reader.

see page 91: **69.** Milton Caniff, **Terry and the Pirates**

**68.** Milton Caniff (1907-1988), **Terry and the Pirates** (October 22, 1934-February 23, 1973) (Caniff's tenure, October 22, 1934 - December 29, 1946). July 2, 1939. Traces of graphite, pasteovers, brush, pen and ink on illustration board, 18 1/8 × 27 1/8 in. (460 × 689 mm). Milton Caniff Collection, The Ohio State University Cartoon Research Library. Copyright © 1939 Tribune Media Services. All rights reserved. Reprinted with permission.

**Evolution of Style II.** Within a year or so, Caniff evolved the chiaroscuro treatment into something considerably more complex than depicting the play of light and shadow. Shadows are still brushed in on the sides of figures and objects away from the light source, but all wrinkles in clothing, for instance, are rendered with heavy brush strokes whether they are on the "shadow side" of a figure or not. And not all the shadow sides are drenched in black; the Dragon Lady's face in Panel 9 as she carries April Kane off, for example, should be shadowed but, for the sake of narrative clar-

ity, is not. Caniff's modification of the technique sustained the same visual effect of high contrast between black and white, but the artwork is now much blacker than earlier. Night scenes like those here are particularly startling, and Caniff delighted in producing such effects as those in the second picture. The Dragon Lady, whose machinations are depicted here, is the most memorable of Caniff's creations, a pirate chieftain so able and ruthless that she fills the hereditary masculine role completely, inspiring her men to call her "Master" despite her obvious feminine attractions. Caniff occasionally suggested that she might prefer being loved by men to leading them, underscoring the mysteriousness of her circumstances with the puzzle of her personality and giving her a psychological depth that made her immensely appealing. Caniff also frequently used humor with dramatic effect, as he does here. The top half of the next-to-last panel is a pasted-over piece of paper upon which Caniff made some adjustment in his drawing for that panel.

**Evolution of Style II.** Irving Berlin's "White Christmas" was in its third season when, in one of the most impressive deployments of his contrastive chiaroscuro, Caniff paused in his storytelling on Christmas Day, 1944, to pay tribute to the pilots who flew supplies over "the hump" from India to the embattled Chinese army in western China. The treatment of the snowy mountain range, however, Caniff said he "stole" from Roy Crane. For the rest of his career, Caniff produced special non-narrative holiday strips: this enabled him to step "out of character" to recognize the achievements of otherwise unsung military people, and it also nicely evaded a continuity problem storytelling cartoonists encountered with newspapers that didn't publish on Christmas Day.

all but vanished from the strip. Crane played the stories for the merriment he could provoke, but not for a daily punch line. He also saw to it that Wash scampers rapidly from one exotic locale to another, engaging in a succession of desperate gambles to strike it rich again and again, and, at the same time, to capture the undying affection of the latest "bonbon" who catches his ever-roving eye. Excitement rather than laughter was the quarry in Crane's pursuit. And in search of it, Wash wanders the world. Then early in 1928, Crane introduced a new kind of character, adding another dimension to the strip and changing it forever.

Bull Dawson is the captain of the ship Wash engages to take him to the latest desert island where a treasure is supposed to be. Dawson is a burly modern version of Long John Silver. Lacking Silver's charming guile, Dawson is evil incarnate: no physical abuse is too savage or murderous for him to inflict, no underhanded trick too vile. Villainy in the strip is now a deadly serious matter. Dawson doesn't fool around. When he beats up Wash, Wash hurts. But the presence of Dawson and others of his ilk did not alter entirely the essential nature of *Wash Tubbs*.

For all the menace of its new crop of villains, the strip remained a boisterous, rollicking, fun-loving strip, full of last-minute dashes, free-for-all fisticuffs, galloping horse chases, pretty girls, and sound effects—Bam, Pow, Boom, Sok, Lickety-whop. Drawn in the traditional "bigfoot" cartoon style, Crane's characters, when they ran, ran all out—knees up to their chins. When they were knocked down in a fight, they flipped backwards, head over heels. But the backgrounds against which they cavorted were increasingly rendered with realistic fidelity to nature. Crane's seascapes are dramatic, the water a brooding solid black with white foam flecking the caps of the waves.

This combination of the fantastic and the authentic—cartoony-looking people capering through realistic scenery, whimsical plots jammed with life-threatening dangers, humorous heroes with real feelings—made *Wash Tubbs* unique on the funnies page (FIGURE 50). The comically rendered characters gave the strip its distinctive appeal and underscored its light-hearted ambiance. No one could take such characters altogether seriously, so the strip radiated a fellowship of carefree excitement and of good times had by all. It was high spirited and often laugh provoking; its sole reason for being, to tell entertaining adventure stories. Infected with a fun-loving spirit, the strip was every boy's dream of what adventure should be—and the dream of every man who still harbored the boy within him. Adventure should be exciting and dangerous, but not too dangerous: the idea was to have some fun in an otherwise mundane life.

Then in May 1929, when Crane brought into the strip the hawk-nosed, flinty-eyed, lantern-jawed vagabond adventurer Captain Easy, he transformed the strip again. Easy is the classic soldier of fortune. He gives his occupation as "beach-comber, boxer, cook, aviator, seaman, explorer, and soldier of artillery, infantry, and cavalry." And he's a champion brawler.

Easy was an inspired invention. A swashbuckler of the old school, Easy wore jodhpurs and boots for most of his early adventures. He looked the part of a footloose adventurer, and he was supremely capable. And he and Wash became friends for life.

Crane quickly developed the over-arching formula by which the strip was henceforth guided: Wash pursued his effervescent dreams of love and wealth until he got himself (and Easy) into trouble; and then Easy, brain clicking and both fists flying, got them out again. And the spirit of fun-loving adventure remained intact (FIGURE 51). Coulton Waugh put it memorably: "In the old days, tubby Tubbs and lanky Easy were loose-footed soldiers of fortune, a big and a little stone rolling through the romantic places of the earth, usually broke, sometimes fabulously wealthy, but always ready for fight, frolic, or feed. The special quality that set off the strip was that it had the appeal of a child's box of fascinating toy soldiers, painted in bright red and green, and marching to battle, all gay and flashing, to the inspiriting rattle of tiny drums." [13]

However much Crane's graphic devices may have attracted the attention and admiration of fellow members of the inky-fingered fraternity, it was Captain Easy that won their unalloyed admiration. Easy

LET'S TAKE A WALK, TERRY...

YES, SIR, COLONEL CORKIN!

I'M GOING TO MAKE A SPEECH—AND IT'LL BE THE LAST ONE OF ITS KIND IN CAPTIVITY—SO DON'T GET A SHORT CIRCUIT BETWEEN THE EARS...

NO, SIR

WELL, YOU MADE IT...YOU'RE A FLIGHT OFFICER IN THE AIR FORCES OF THE ARMY OF THE UNITED STATES...THOSE WINGS ARE LIKE A NEON LIGHT ON YOUR CHEST...I'M NOT GOING TO WAVE THE FLAG AT YOU—BUT SOME THINGS YOU MUST NEVER FORGET...

...EVERY COUNTRY HAS HAD A HAND IN THE DEVELOPMENT OF THE AIRPLANE—BUT, AFTER ALL, THE WRIGHT BROTHERS WERE A COUPLE OF DAYTON, OHIO, BOYS—AND KITTY HAWK IS STRICTLY IN NORTH CAROLINA... THE HALLMARK OF THE UNITED STATES IS ON EVERY AIRCRAFT..

...SO YOU FIND YOURSELF IN A POSITION TO DEFEND THE COUNTRY THAT GAVE YOU THE WEAPON WITH WHICH TO DO IT... BUT IT WASN'T JUST YOU WHO EARNED THOSE WINGS... A GHOSTLY ECHELON OF GOOD GUYS FLEW THEIR HEARTS OUT IN OLD KITES TO GIVE YOU THE KNOW-HOW...

...AND SOME SMART SLIDE RULE JOKERS SWEAT IT OUT OVER DRAWING BOARDS TO GIVE YOU A MACHINE THAT WILL KEEP YOU UP THERE SHOOTING ... I RECOMMENDED YOU FOR FIGHTER AIRCRAFT AND I WANT YOU TO BE COCKY AND SMART AND PROUD OF BEING A BUZZ-BOY...

...BUT DON'T FORGET THAT EVERY BULLET YOU SHOOT, EVERY GALLON OF GAS AND OIL YOU BURN WAS BROUGHT HERE BY TRANSPORT PILOTS WHO FLEW IT IN OVER THE WORST TERRAIN IN THE WORLD! YOU MAY GET THE GLORY—BUT THEY PUT THE LIFT IN YOUR BALLOON!...

...AND DON'T LET ME EVER CATCH YOU BEING HIGH-BICYCLE WITH THE ENLISTED MEN IN YOUR GROUND CREW! WITHOUT THEM, YOU'D NEVER GET TEN FEET OFF THE GROUND! EVERY GREASE MONKEY IN THAT GANG IS RIGHT BESIDE YOU IN THE COCKPIT— AND THEIR HANDS ARE ON THAT STICK, JUST THE SAME AS YOURS...

...YOU'LL GET ANGRY AS THE DEVIL AT THE ARMY AND ITS SO-CALLED RED TAPE...BUT BE PATIENT WITH IT... SOMEHOW, THE OLD EAGLE HAS MANAGED TO END UP IN POSSESSION OF THE BALL IN EVERY WAR SINCE 1776—SO JUST HUMOR IT ALONG...

OKAY, SPORT, END OF SPEECH...WHEN YOU GET UP IN THAT "WILD BLUE YONDER" THE SONG TALKS ABOUT—REMEMBER, THERE ARE A LOT OF GOOD GUYS MISSING FROM MESS TABLES IN THE SOUTH PACIFIC, ALASKA, AFRICA, BRITAIN, ASIA AND BACK HOME WHO ARE SORTA COUNTING ON YOU TO TAKE IT FROM HERE! GOOD NIGHT, KID!

**71.** Milton Caniff (1907 - 1988), **Male Call** (January 24, 1943 - March 3, 1946). March 5, 1944. Traces of graphite, brush, pen and ink on illustration board, 6 x 21¾ in. (152 x 556 mm). Milton Caniff Collection, The Ohio State University Cartoon Research Library. MALE CALL Copyright March 5, 1944. Reprinted by permission of the Milton Caniff Estate.

Another of Caniff's famous creations came about through one of his numerous contributions to the war effort during World War II. Intended to remind soldiers what they were fighting for, Miss Lace, a curvaceous bundle of camaraderie, was the central figure (so to speak), of *Male Call,* a mildly risqué weekly comic strip he drew without remuneration for distribution as a morale-booster to camp and unit newspapers. Immensely popular, the strip was distributed by the Camp Newspaper Service, a military syndicate, and appeared in more than 3,000 papers, the greatest circulation in number of individual publications ever attained by any comic strip.

inspired a generation of cartoonists. Milton Caniff, for instance, was an early fan. And when he came to do his own strip at the Associated Press in 1933 *(Dickie Dare,* whose youthful protagonist dreams himself into adventures with the heroes of the books he reads, *Robin Hood* and *Robinson Crusoe),* Caniff eventually introduced an "Easy" of his own into the strip, "Dynamite Dan" Flynn, who takes Dickie out of his dreamland into the real world of adventure. Pat Ryan in *Terry and the Pirates* was Easy in yet another incarnation. As was Uncle Phil in Mel Graff's *Patsy* and Slam Bradley in the comic book adventures created by Jerry Siegel and Joe Shuster before they created Superman (who, in turn, looks like Slam Bradley, thereby completing the chain back to Crane). But before these imitations took hold on the public's fancy, another development in the form of the comic strip took place. Illustrators invaded the comics pages of the nation's newspapers.

Illustrators drew everything with nearly photographic realism. And this development enhanced the appeal of the adventure strip: the realistic visuals made the genre's inherent suspense keener by making the people and the events seem real.

Among the earliest attempts at realistic rendering in comics was *Tailspin Tommy,* a strip that sought to capitalize on the public interest in aviation in the wake of Charles Lindbergh's heroic solo flight across the Atlantic. Starting July 19, 1928 (just about a year after "Lucky" Lindy's historic flight), *Tailspin Tommy* was drawn by Hal Forrest, whose style, we might say, was "little foot" cartoony: it tried for illustrative realism, but its line work was too clumsy to achieve the desired effect. Forrest later embellished his work with cross-hatching and other shading effects, but that merely emphasized the weakness of his draftsmanship

**72.** Frank Miller (1898-1949), **Barney Baxter** (about 1935 - January 1950). October 21, 1942. Pen and ink on illustration board, 5 × 20 in. (128 × 508 mm). Collection of the Cartoon Art Museum, San Francisco. Copyright © 1942. Reprinted with special permission of King Features Syndicate.

Because his hero was a freelance pilot, Miller was able to get his strip into World War II faster than most. He managed to have Barney bombing Tokyo on the same day in April 1942 as Jimmy Doolittle made his famous raid on the Japanese capital. (No small feat considering that the strip in question was produced six to eight weeks before its publication date!) Miller's caricatures of the Japanese foe were particularly monstrous, but his shading of his artwork with elaborate hachuring made his strip one of the most unusual visual treats around.

(FIGURE 53). Most other early experiments in illustration were similarly flawed by the artists' relative ineptitude. Then January dawned in 1929.

January 7, 1929, is a date often cited as the official inauguration date for the adventure strip. *Buck Rogers* began on that day; and so did *Tarzan*. But it wasn't the adventure strip that began that January: as we've seen, Roy Crane had been doing an adventure strip for several years by then. No, January 7, 1929 was, rather, the day that illustrators arrived in the comics. On that auspicious date, thirteen newspapers in the United States and two in Canada introduced an impressively illustrated new strip, an interpretation of Edgar Rice Burroughs' *Tarzan* by Harold R. Foster. Foster was in advertising, and one of his clients was Joseph H. Neebe, who had formed a company called Famous Books and Plays for the purpose of adapting and selling serialized pictorial versions of prose works to newspapers. When Neebe couldn't get *Tarzan's* best known illustrator, J. Allen St. John, to do the adaptation, he turned to Foster. Foster produced a ten-week continuity, sixty daily installments consisting of illustrations with typeset narrative prose running beneath the pictures. While this effort was not, technically, a comic strip (the pictures did not contain any speech balloons), Foster used the comic strip form—a sequence of pictures running horizontally across the newspaper page. And Foster was a superbly accomplished artist. His drawing of anatomy was flawless; his technique clean and crisp. The clumsy attempts at illustration by other comic strip artists of the day were immediately eclipsed by Foster's virtuoso performance.

After the ten-week run, Foster returned to advertising art, and the subsequent newspaper comic strip

**73.** Milton Caniff (1907-1988), **Steve Canyon** (January 13, 1947-June 5, 1988). July 20, 1947. Traces of graphite, white gouache, pasteovers, brush, pen and ink on illustration board, 16 1/2 × 24 1/8 in. (419 × 613 mm). Milton Caniff Collection, The Ohio State University Cartoon Research Library. STEVE CANYON Copyright July 20, 1947. Reprinted by permission of the Milton Caniff Estate.

Caniff abandoned *Terry and the Pirates* in 1946 in order to produce a new strip, *Steve Canyon*, that he would own and control absolutely himself. Ex-serviceman Canyon was an older, more worldly-wise version of Terry, but he was firmly rooted in American, not Oriental, tradition. Caniff invoked the formula of the Western in devising his new creation: Canyon was a well-traveled, knowledgeable pilot,

a "planesman" in the lineage of a scout on the plains of the West; Caniff even gave him a grizzled old sidekick, Happy Easter (patterned after the durable Gabby Hayes), who here proves himself as much a heroic figure as the strip's title character. The third-to-last panel includes two tiny figures—on the right, Steve Canyon; on the left, a police officer. The yellow-brown square over the latter is a glue stain that indicates where a pasted-over correction was applied. The correction (which appears in the published version of this installment) was a smaller rendition of the policeman, putting him further into the background than Canyon and thereby giving even greater depth to the composition of the panel.

**74.** George Wunder (1912-1987), **Terry and the Pirates** (October 22, 1934 - February 23, 1973). June 26, 1948. Traces of graphite, brush, pen and ink on illustration board, 6½ × 21¾ in. (165 × 552 mm). Collection of Jim Scancarelli. Copyright © 1948 Tribune Media Services. All rights reserved. Reprinted with permission.

It was a wholly unknown artist in the Associated Press bullpen who would attempt the impossible, succeeding Caniff on *Terry and the Pirates*. Imitating Caniff's drawing style with great panache, Wunder made a spectacular start on December 30, 1946, and went on to achieve (almost) the impossible for the next twenty-six years, well over twice the length of Caniff's term on the feature.

adaptations of Burroughs' Tarzan books were done by Rex Maxon, whose ability was somewhat less than Foster's. By 1931, however, the Depression had cut substantially into Foster's income, and when he was offered the chance to return to *Tarzan,* this time to illustrate a Sunday page, he seized the opportunity. Given the small number of papers that had published the 1929 daily series, it is undoubtedly Foster's stint on the more widely circulated Sunday *Tarzan* from September 17,1931 to May 2, 1937 that proved so influential in comics (FIGURE 55).

Even so, Foster was more admired than imitated outright. His impact was not achieved by providing an example that could be copied in any slavish way. His influence was simpler, more direct: he showed what quality illustration could do to enhance the narrative drama of adventure strips. And beginning February 13, 1937, he showed his talent in *Prince Valiant,* a painstakingly executed re-creation of medieval Europe, when knighthood was in flower (FIGURES 60-61). After Foster, the field was suddenly open to accomplished illustrators, who had, quite possibly, scorned comic strips before.

Perhaps the most impressive of the illustrators who came to the comics pages after Foster was Alex Raymond (whose work Foster greatly admired, just as Raymond admired Foster's). Raymond had been working as an order clerk in a Wall Street brokerage when the market crashed in October 1929. Suddenly out of work, he fell back on his drawing ability to earn a living, eventually assisting in the King Features bull pen. He also drew some of Chic Young's *Blondie* (notably, the heroine's wedding); by 1933, he was drawing Lyman Young's (Chic's brother) aviation-adventure strip (which had begun August 13, 1928, as one of those imitation *Annie* sagas), *Tim Tyler's Luck* (FIGURE 54), deploying a slick illustrative style.

Raymond would achieve lasting fame with the strip King Features soon contracted him to do. This

Robbins' style, which he said he arrived at independently, is clearly in the Caniff tradition with its heavy use of black for shadows, but Robbins' lush brushwork is his own. *Johnny Hazard* was intended by its syndicate to compete with *Terry and the Pirates,* and Hazard began syndicated life as a pilot in China in the closing days of World War II. After the war, he became something of a freelance trouble-shooter and roamed the world.

was *Flash Gordon,* beginning on Sunday, January 7, 1934. At the same time as he drew this space opera epic, Raymond also did *Jungle Jim* (printed as the top tier, or "topper," on the *Flash* page), and a daily detective-style strip, *Secret Agent X-9* (which Raymond abandoned in the fall of 1935 in order to concentrate on the other two ventures). Both *X-9* and *Jungle Jim* were stylishly rendered, but in *Flash Gordon,* Raymond created life—a mythical world peopled by personages more beautiful, handsomer, more graceful than any anywhere else (FIGURES 57-58). The stories (written by Don Moore) gave the characters little personality, but the beauty of Raymond's visuals seduced his readers into believing in the characters and their adventures. Seldom has the illustrative power of an artist to persuade received such ringing testimony.

Meanwhile, another cartoonist was creating a sensation with artwork that only approached realism. Until the debut of *Dick Tracy* on October 4, 1931, the continuity strip had focused on one of two extremes, exotic adventure or domestic intrigue. *Tracy* brought the excitement of adventure to readers' front doors when Chester Gould's plainclothes cop started fighting contemporary crime in everyone's home town. Gould came to Chicago in 1921 to attend Northwestern University, and he also began inventing comic strips. He kept it up for the next ten years, submitting nearly sixty ideas, he later said, and selling one every now and then, but nothing ran for long. Finally, simmering with anger at the lawlessness of the Prohibition era, Gould bethought himself of the kind of hero who would rescue America—"a symbol," as Gould said, "of law and order who could dish it out to the underworld exactly as they dished it out, only better." Gould appropriated the hard-boiled detective persona from the pulp fiction of the day and, in visualizing him, gave him the chiseled profile he associated with Sherlock Holmes (FIGURE 62). It was the

**76.** Ken Ernst (1918-1985), **Mary Worth** (Originally entitled *Apple Mary*) (about 1934- Present). March 25, 1945. Traces of graphite, brush, pen and ink on illustration board, 13 × 21 in. (330 × 273 mm). Collection of Robert Stolzer. Copyright © 1945. Reprinted with special permission of King Features Syndicate.

Starting on the strip in 1942, Ernst applied his slick illustrative technique and, with writer Allen Saunders, made Mary Worth the preeminent soap opera strip on the comics page for his entire tenure on the feature. Although influenced initially by Caniff, Ernst's drawing style veered off on its own as it matured.

**77.** Raeburn Van Buren (1891-1987), **Abbie an' Slats** (July 7, 1937-January 30, 1971). March 19, 1945. Traces of graphite, pen and ink on illustration board, 4 7/8 × 19 1/8 in. (124 × 486 mm). Collection of Mark J. Cohen and Rose Marie McDaniel. Copyright © 1945. ABBIE N' SLATS reprinted by permission of United Feature Syndicate, Inc.

Created by cartoonist Al Capp (mostly as a maneuver that would give him leverage in negotiating with his syndicate about his share of *Li'l Abner*), *Abbie an' Slats* (a comedic soap opera about a spinster lady and her rough-edged nephew) was drawn by a distinguished magazine illustrator, who Capp was able to persuade into taking the assignment by convincing him that radio would destroy the magazine illustration market. In adapting his painterly magazine style to the demands of linear black-and-white for newspaper reproduction, Van Buren created a rustic-looking style all his own, illustrative but capable of comic exaggeration, too. After Capp won his negotiating bout, he turned the writing of the strip over to his brother Elliot Caplin.

beginning of raw violence on the comics page. No comic strip had previously shown gunplay and bloodshed; within a couple years, a half-dozen imitators were trading hot lead in the funnies. But Tracy was more than a shoot-'em-up specialist. Gould began working closely with Chicago police, incorporating authentic procedural techniques into his strip (FIGURE 63). But in creating villains for his hero, he departed dramatically from reality to create a gallery of ghoulish crooks, caricatures of evil that underscored the moral of his strip: crime doesn't pay, and a life of crime will put you in daily communion with such creatures as these: Pruneface, Flattop, the Mole, Shoulders, BB Eyes, the Brow, Shakey, Mumbles. Gould's creation would come to share a place in the history of detective fiction hitherto occupied in solitude by Conan Doyle's Sherlock Holmes. And in the copycat history of newspaper comic strips, *Dick Tracy* may be the most imitated of all.

The last chapter in the evolution of the adventure strip was written by Milton Caniff in his classic tale of Oriental intrigue, *Terry and the Pirates*. When the strip was introduced October 22, 1934, it was a competent but not particularly distinguished offering, rendered in the "little foot" manner: simple linework, realistically deployed but not much embellished with illustrative detail (FIGURE 65). But in the next couple years as the young Terry Lee and his vagabond mentor, Pat Ryan, encounter such picturesque and compelling creations as the Dragon Lady (a gorgeous but ruthless pirate queen) and Burma (a beautiful fugitive), Caniff virtually redefined the genre. Although not, strictly speaking, an illustrator, he perfected a technique of realistic rendering that revolutionized comic strip illustration (FIGURE 66). As a storyteller,

( C O N T I N U E D   P A G E   1 0 6 )

**78.** Dale Messick (Born 1904), **Brenda Starr** (June 30, 1940-Present). December 30, 1945. Watercolor, pen and ink on illustration board, 12 ½ × 28 in. (318 × 711 mm). Collection of Mark J. Cohen and Rose Marie McDaniel. Copyright © 1945 Tribune Media Services. All rights reserved. Reprinted with permission.

Brenda, the star reporter on a metropolitan newspaper, represented the ultimate in female liberation when she first appeared. Messick initially proposed an adventure strip about a lady bandit, but that, apparently, was a bit too liberated.

Illustrated in a glamorous (and sometimes even frilly) manner, the strip manages to present its heroine as an adventuress both sexy and superbly independent (except that she pines for her "Mystery Man," Basil St. John, who raises black orchids and drifts in and out of the strip, disappearing for months at a time). The artwork here has been hand colored for exhibition purposes; and the pin-up panel, from a different date, has been joined to this strip for the same purpose.

**79.** Ham Fisher (1901-1955), **Joe Palooka** (April 1930-1984). September 13, 19(50?). Blue pencil, brush, pen and ink on illustration board, 5 ⅞ × 19 ⅞ in. (149 × 505 mm). From the Permanent Collection of the International Museum of Cartoon Art, Boca Raton. Copyright © McNaught Syndicate, Inc.

One of the few successful, long-running strips to focus on sports, *Joe Palooka* was, for a time, one of the top five comic strips in the country. Fisher designed his prize-fighting protagonist as an all-American hero—wholesome, good-hearted, and principled to a fault, as well as strong. His boxing matches were usually attended by real-life dignitaries, whom Fisher drew into ringside seats; at least two Presidents of the United States made appearances in the strip: "Truman" appears here. Light blue shading indicates where engravers should create gray tone with Ben-Day dot pattern.

*opposite:* **80.** Fred Harman (1902-1988?), **Red Ryder** (November 6, 1938-December 1964). March 16, 1941. Traces of blue pencil, pasteovers, white gouache, brush, pen and ink on illustration board, 28 × 21½ in. (711 × 546 mm). Collection of Jim Scancarelli. Copyright © 1941 McNaught Syndicate, Inc.

Considering that the mythology of the nation resides in the Old West, there have been surprisingly few comic strips set in that milieu. Harman's *Red Ryder,* however, was one of the best—and the longest lasting. A lineal descendant of an earlier Harman effort called *Bronc Peeler* (which Harman syndicated himself), *Red Ryder* was illustrated in an authentically raw-boned manner with a bold and fluid brush stroke that imbued the action with energy and ambiance. Two of the panels on this Sunday page have been reconstructed by cartoonist Jim Scancarelli (the first panel and the close-up of the horse).

*see page 102:* **79.** Ham Fisher, **Joe Palooka**

**81.** Warren Tufts (1925-1982), **Casey Ruggles** (May 1949-October 1955). June 22, 1953. Brush, pen and ink on illustration board, 4 1/4 × 15 3/8 in. (108 × 137 mm). Collection of Mark J. Cohen and Rose Marie McDaniel. Copyright © 1953. CASEY RUGGLES reprinted by permission of United Feature Syndicate, Inc.

Illustrated in the manner of Alex Raymond, *Casey Ruggles* was a meticulously researched and painstakingly rendered Western. Tufts maintained that it took him eighty hours a week. Eventually, he could not sustain the quality and quit the strip in the summer of 1954. Other hands continued it briefly.

he infused the most exotic of tales with palpable realism. And he enhanced the drama of the traditional adventure story formula by incorporating character development into the action-packed plots.

Influenced by his studio-mate, Noel Sickles, who was doing *Scorchy Smith,* an aviation strip in the Associated Press feature lineup (Figure 64), Caniff began to employ an impressionistic chiaroscuro graphic technique that defined shapes with shadows rather than lines. It saved time (because he didn't have to draw every wrinkle in clothing and every background detail) without sacrificing the illusion of reality (Figure 67). To further promote that illusion, Caniff sought absolute authenticity in the visual details of his panels. But his signal achievement as a cartoonist lay in his storytelling sense.

Adventure strips of the day traded chiefly in exotic situations and physical danger and spent little energy on characterization. Caniff, an avid student of the theater, began attending to the personalities of his characters as well as to the technique of his visuals. Almost from the beginning, his plots are driven by his characters, whose desires and flaws determine motivation and outcome. Events and people interact, one feeding off the other in a reciprocating cause-and-effect relationship. His stories thus invariably create suspense on at least two levels at once: we want to know what will happen, and we want to know how the people involved will react, develop, change and/or grow. Simply stated, Caniff's accomplishment was to make us avidly interested in his people as well as their adventures. In *Terry and the Pirates,* Caniff set new standards of excellence for the adventure strip, and all subsequent forays into the field would be measured in one way or another against his achievement.

Caniff reached the pinnacle of his fame during World War II. In the strip, Terry joined the Army Air Force, and Caniff's realistic and sympathetic treatment of military life championed the achievements of

**82.** Leonard Starr (Born 1925), **Mary Perkins On Stage** (February 10, 1957-1979). September 17, 1969. Traces of graphite, pen and ink on illustration board, 5 × 16 1/2 in. (127 × 419 mm). Collection of Mark J. Cohen and Rose Marie McDaniel. Copyright © 1969 Tribune Media Services. All rights reserved. Reprinted with permission.

An outstanding example of soap opera, the chronicle of the life and career of a young actress named Mary Perkins, Starr's strip was produced in the highest illustrative traditions of the medium. The stories reeked of authentic stagecraft and lingo.

ordinary men and women in uniform. The cartoonist became an American Kipling. Terry's trenchant, pragmatic patriotism warmed hearts and steeled nerves on the home front as well as at the battlefront (FIGURE 69). The Sunday page for October 17, 1943, so incisively captured the wartime spirit of the times that it was read into the Congressional Record to become a part of the national archive (FIGURE 70).

Other cartoonists working in the realm of realism also sent their comic strip heroes to war: Ham Fisher sent Joe Palooka (FIGURE 79); Frank Miller, Barney Baxter (FIGURE 72); Zack Mosley, Smilin' Jack; Lank Leonard, Mickey Finn. Even the protagonists of some of the humorous strips went—Barney Google went into the Navy; Snuffy Smith and Skeezix, the Army; Tillie the Toiler, the WACs. Andy Gump and Superman were both rejected for service. Andy was too old; Superman failed the eye test because, with his X-ray vision, he read the eye chart on the wall two rooms away from him. Superman stayed home and fought spies and saboteurs, and so did Dick Tracy and his legions of imitators.

After the war, Caniff caused a new sensation: he abandoned *Terry and the Pirates,* which was owned by the Chicago Tribune-New York Daily News Syndicate, to create a new strip for Field Enterprises, *Steve Canyon,* one which he would own himself (FIGURE 73). Even Caniff found that his new creation would be measured against the standards he himself had set with Terry, as long ago as before the war.

Perhaps the most difficult of the measuring-up tasks, however, was faced by George Wunder, who took over Caniff's *Terry and the Pirates.* With Caniff still working his magic, often on the same page of the newspaper, Wunder's work understandably suffered by comparison; but if his *Terry* is evaluated solely on its own merits, it stands as a superb achievement in both story and art (FIGURE 74).

The continuity strip in the thirties and forties blossomed in genre other than adventure, too. In 1934,

(CONTINUED PAGE 110)

**83.** Stan Drake (1921-1997), **The Heart of Juliet Jones** (March 9, 1953- Present ). April 20, 1969. Trace of blue pencil, pasteovers, brush, pen and ink on illustration board, 12¼ × 17⅜ in. (311 × 441 mm). Collection of the Cartoon Art Museum, San Francisco. Copyright © 1969. Reprinted with special permission of King Features Syndicate.

One of the best of the post-war illustrative soap opera entries, *Juliet Jones* was written by Elliot Caplin and drawn with a masterful hand by Drake. Drake composed panels with attention to dramatic emphasis and visual variety, and when he feathered the soft edges of wrinkles in clothing, he invariably made the cloth appear to be the softest cashmere. The machinery in the third panel is probably traced from a photograph; it was done on a separate piece of paper that was then pasted into the artwork.

**84.** Alex Kotzky (1923-1996), **Apartment 3-G** (May 8, 1961-Present). December 10, 1967. Traces of graphite, pasteovers, white gouache, pen and ink on illustration baord, 13 7/8 × 20 1/8 in. (352 × 511 mm). Collection of Frank Pauer. Copyright © 1967. Reprinted with special permission of King Features Syndicate.

Another fine example of the illustrator's craft, the soap opera of *Apartment 3-G* rotates adventures among a repertory company of three young career women who share the same apartment. Working from scripts by writer Nick Dallis, Kotzky drew his heroines with great skill (here, Margo and Lu Ann): not only do they look beautiful, but they look different from one another, and Kotzky could even draw them recognizably with different expressions. As comic strips began to be reproduced at smaller and smaller sizes, storytelling strips often became little more than panel after panel of "talking heads," and here Kotzky's talent gave distinction to his strip.

**85.** Al Williamson (Born 1931), **Secret Agent X-9** (January 22, 1934-Present). February 22, 1973. Blue pencil, brush, pen and ink on illustration board, 5 3/4 x 19 3/4 in. (146 x 502 mm). Courtesy of the artist. Copyright © 1973. Reprinted with special permission of King Features Syndicate.

Beginning in 1967, Williamson was able to continue one of the comic strips launched by the cartoonist whose work he admired most, Alex Raymond. The syndicate renamed Raymond's seminal strip *Secret Agent Corrigan;* although Williamson and writer Archie Goodwin objected to the change, for the next dozen years they produced a dazzlingly sophisticated version of Raymond's brainchild. Williamson's art, sometimes evocative of Raymond's, goes the master one better in its truly stunning use of solid blacks that give the work a liquid sheen unlike any other on the comics page.

Martha Orr concocted *Apple Mary.* Inspired by the Frank Capra movie *Lady for a Day,* about a colorful Damon Runyonesque street peddler named Apple Annie, Orr's strip followed the adventures of another street merchant as she encountered all kinds of evildoers. When Orr retired in 1939, the writing of the strip was taken over by Allen Saunders, who changed the name of the strip to *Mary Worth* and made the protagonist a sort of grandmotherly referee in the domestic travails of others (FIGURE 76). And with that, the champion soap opera strip emerged. Others followed. *Abbie an' Slats* (July 7, 1937, FIGURE 77), *Rex Morgan, M.D.* (May 10, 1948), and *Judge Parker* (November 1952), to name a few of the most enduring. Among the most impressively illustrated were Leonard Starr's *On Stage* (February 10, 1957, FIGURE 82), Stan Drake's *The Heart of Juliet Jones* (March 9, 1953, FIGURE 83), and Alex Kotsky's *Apartment 3-G* (May 8, 1961, FIGURE 84). With such work in print, Al Capp was justified in saying (as he did) that the best illustration in America at the time was taking place on the comics pages of the nation's newspapers.

Martha Orr was not the first woman cartoonist, but the most famous of the distaff side is probably Dale Messick, who changed her name from Dalia in order to mask her gender so she could sell her work to a predominantly male editorial world. The work in question, *Brenda Starr,* was an adventure strip with a pronounced interest in women's fashion and hair styles; inaugurated June 30, 1940, it proved its appeal by lasting through the end of the century (FIGURE 78).

Other illustrative adventure strips poured onto the comics pages towards the end of World War II and immediately thereafter. Frank Robbins produced one of the best in the Caniff mold, *Johnny Hazard* (June 5, 1944, FIGURE 75), about a pilot (like Terry). Other strips about ex-servicemen turned trouble-

**86.** Al Williamson (Born 1931), **Star Wars** (March 11, 1979-March 11, 1984). February 26, 1984. Traces of graphite, blue pencil, pasteover, applied half-tone film, brush, pen and ink on illustration board, 14 ¾ × 22 ¼ in. (375 × 565 mm). Courtesy of the artist. Copyright © 1984 Lucasfilm Ltd. (LFL).

Just as the space operas *Buck Rogers* and *Flash Gordon* had stood at the very beginning of the era of adventure strips, so does *Star Wars* stand at the very end.

Based upon George Lucas's popular film series, this may be "the last adventure strip" to be launched (as Williamson asserts). According to report, Lucas was going to pull the plug on the strip a month or so earlier, but when he noticed that it was almost the anniversary of the strip's beginning, he authorized Williamson and his writing partner Goodwin to do one more story so it could end on the same month and day it began.

shooter included *Bruce Gentry* by a Caniff assistant, Ray Bailey (March 25, 1945), *Hank* by Coulton Waugh (April 30, 1945), and *Rip Kirby*, Alex Raymond's masterful postwar effort about a sophisticated private detective (March 4, 1946, FIGURE 59). Although born before the War (November 6, 1938), Fred Harman's *Red Ryder* gave the West a flamboyant but somehow gnarly reality (FIGURE 80); another Western, Warren Tufts' *Casey Ruggles* (May 22, 1949, FIGURE 81), was much more in the slick illustrative tradition of Alex Raymond.

All of these, whether soap operas or adventures, were descendants of the work of Foster, Raymond, and Caniff—and Crane, their mutual inspiration—in the 1930s. By the end of that crucial decade in the history of the medium, the scope as well as the form of the comic strip had been well established. Comic strips were unabashedly intended as entertainment, offering up jokes, adventure, or heartthrob. Before the decade ended, however, one more ingredient had been added to the traditional scope. Satire. Social and political commentary. We'll return to this development anon. But first, an interlude with infinite jest. ●

## Launching a Legend

*Steve Canyon* hove into public view on the crest of a wave of unequaled ballyhoo, the culmination of a promotional campaign unique in both its length and content. The news that Caniff would start a new adventure comic strip broke in early 1945, when he still had two years to go on his *Terry* contract. Since he was leaving the Tribune-News Syndicate chiefly to gain control and complete ownership of his new strip, Caniff would do nothing during that two-year period to endanger his future proprietary rights: he didn't draw a line on the new strip until his old contract expired on October 15, 1946. So the new Caniff creation was sold solely on the basis of its creator's reputation. And that was apparently enough for an unprecedented number of editors. On January 13, 1947, *Canyon* began in 234 newspapers, 162 of which had bought the feature before seeing even the earliest promotional drawings of the characters that had appeared only seven weeks previously.

Even with the strip's debut, Caniff continued to deny his audience a glimpse of the character they'd been waiting so long to see: perhaps indulging an impish sense of humor, the master storyteller built suspense during the strip's first week through the chancy device

of keeping his hero offstage. What readers finally saw was a tall, lean, square-jawed, hawk-nosed worldly-wise soldier of fortune. In personality, he was an older, more mature Terry, but Caniff had taken pains to make him look markedly different, giving him a theatrical dark streak in his blond hair—a feature of his appearance that excited great comment in the promotional materials. Deliberately contrived to appeal to a post-war audience of veterans, Canyon was an ex-Army Transport Command pilot, and, like thousands of others, he had set himself up in business—operating his own cargo airline. His vocation gave him a plausible excuse for going anywhere and doing anything, and Caniff gave the airline a name to match that promise—Horizons Unlimited. When the Korean War broke out, Caniff put Canyon back in uniform, and, like Terry before him, the character became a spokesman for military men for the remainder of the strip's run. It was a maneuver that eventually proved disastrous: during the unpopular Vietnam War a generation later, *Steve Canyon* was dropped by most of the papers that published it because of its apparent warlike attitude.

# Of Infinite Jest:
# A Gag-a-Day

## MOVEMENT 4

DESPITE THE FLURRY of postwar comic strip creations in a serious, illustrative mode, the heyday of the continuity strip was already over. "We didn't realize it at the time," Milton Caniff once told me, "but comic strips—particularly continuity strips—were in trouble. Up to then, we had had such a run of popularity that we had begun to believe our own press agents. But Harry Baker [a syndicate official], who was out there selling features, brought us back to reality. He said, 'It's going to go downhill from here on; television's going to take over.' And we thought he was out of his mind. He wasn't. He was absolutely right. But we didn''t realize it at the time. And he said, 'Already people are no longer talking about comic strip characters over lunch; they're talking about Milton Berle, and Burns and Allen, and Jack Benny.' The early television stars were already taking the ball. It didn't happen overnight. It took a long time for it to happen. But it happened." [14]

In the world of cartooning in the fall of 1950, two watershed events began a trickle-down of consequences that would one day divide all that went before from what was yet to come. The first of these events that history and hindsight invest with portent occurred on September 4: on that date, a comic strip by Mort Walker called *Beetle Bailey* began its run (FIGURE 89). It appeared in only twelve papers, a painfully inauspicious beginning. And its circulation didn't improve much over the next six months. By the end of February 1951, it claimed only 25 subscribing papers. But in time, *Beetle Bailey* would become one of the half-dozen most widely distributed comic strips in history. The other strip whose debut marked the fall of 1950 as a turning point in the history of the medium was *Peanuts* (FIGURE 87).

Charles Schulz's colossally successfully strip about introspective "li'l folks" (his original title for the strip) had an even more unspectacular start than *Beetle Bailey*: only seven papers ran the earliest strips, beginning October 2. And its circulation was still well under 100 papers a year later. But within the decade,

**87.** Charles Schulz (Born 1922), **Peanuts** (October 2, 1950-Present). June 4, 1958. Traces of graphite, pen and ink on illustration board, 5½ × 27¼ in. (140 × 692 mm). Herban-Livingston Collection, The Ohio State University Cartoon Research Library. Copyright © 1958. PEANUTS reprinted by permission of United Feature Syndicate, Inc.

Schulz began a revolution in 1950 with his simply-drawn strip about diminutive kids with large round heads who talked in an astonishingly adult manner. The success of *Peanuts* demonstrated to the satisfaction of most newspaper editors and syndicate executives that the reading public wanted a laugh-a-day in their comic strips, not adventure or continuing stories.

**88.** Charles Schulz (Born 1922), **Peanuts** (October 2, 1950 - Present). September 6, 1987. Traces of graphite, white gouache, pasteover, pen and ink on illustration board, 14¾ × 22⅜ in. (375 × 568 mm). Collection of Mark J. Cohen and Rose Marie McDaniel. Copyright © 1987. PEANUTS reprinted by permission of United Feature Syndicate, Inc.

The engaging charm of *Peanuts* stems not from the difference between the worlds of children and adults but from their similarities. The strip's protagonist, the perpetual loser Charlie Brown, has a pet beagle, and when Snoopy begins pursuing activities normally associated with humans (like writing novels, for instance), the humor continues to arise from the unexpected: we don't expect a dog to think like a human, an often petulant one at that, but we see our own fantasies in Snoopy's.

**89.** Mort Walker (Born 1923), **Beetle Bailey** (September 4, 1950 - Present). December 5, 1950. Traces of graphite, applied half-tone film, pen and ink on illustration board, 5 5/8 × 18 5/8 in. (143 × 473 mm). From the Permanent Collection of the International Museum of Cartoon Art, Boca Raton. Copyright © 1950. Reprinted with special permission of King Features Syndicate.

Beetle started syndicated life as a college student—lazy and defiant of authority. When Walker realized that many college students were on the cusp of being inducted into military service for the Korean War, he got Beetle drafted, and the strip's circulation soared.

it would become one of the nation's most popular comics. And it would revolutionize comic strip art: Schulz's deceptively simple style set a new fashion for newspaper cartoonists. And Walker's equally simple but geometrically distinctive style gave cartoonists another model on the funny pages of the coming decades. But the milestone marked by the launching of these two strips had more to do with content than with style.

Both strips told jokes, not stories. They ended each installment with a punch line. Although a week's run of strips might have a common theme, there was no story line. With the success of Walker and Schulz and their imitators, and of others like Hank Ketcham, whose gag panel cartoon *Dennis the Menace* (FIGURE 91) began March 12, 1951 (and was immediately a smash hit), the humorous function of cartooning would emerge during the fifties into pace-setting popularity once again after a quarter-of-a-century hiatus throughout which story strips had held nearly absolute sway.

By the end of the decade, story strips were virtually swept off the comics pages by a deluge of their chortling brethren. But it wasn't fratricide: story strips weren't done in by gag strips. The culprit, as Caniff just told us, was in that box in the living room. Television, which could be seen coast-to-coast by the mid-fifties, displaced radio and the daily newspaper as the nation's source of entertainment in the home. Newspaper editors were desperate to preserve some remnant of their former hold upon the American public. First they fought television, refusing to give up space for any coverage beyond the most cryptic program listings. But when they saw that stories about television increased their readership and circulation, they devoted more space to television news. Elsewhere in the paper, they sought to provide features and services that readers could not find in their television sets. And when it came to the funnies page, the continuity

( CONTINUED PAGE 119 )

**90.** Mort Walker (Born 1923), **Beetle Bailey** (September 4, 1950 - Present). September 24, 1978. Traces of graphite, pasteover, pen and ink on illustration board, 9 x 13 1/4 in. (229 x 337 mm). From the Permanent Collection of the International Museum of Cartoon Art, Boca Raton. Copyright © 1978. Reprinted with special permission of King Features Syndicate.

By the time the strip was a dozen years old, Walker had abstracted human anatomy into bundles of geometric shapes, the orchestration of which was capable of creating greatly exaggerated motion and expression. Beetle is still lazy, still defiant of authority, and the strip as a thematic whole represents an assault on social hierarchies which always have the most incompetent at the top of the heap.

**91.** Hank Ketcham (Born 1920), **Dennis the Menace** (March 12, 1951- Present). July 26, 1992. White gouache, pasteovers, pen and ink on illustration board, 13 5/8 × 19 1/4 in. (346 × 489 mm). Collection of Mark J. Cohen and Rose Marie McDaniel. Copyright © 1992. Reprinted with special permission of King Features Syndicate.

A supremely unique stylist in black and white, Ketcham was another fugitive from the ranks of magazine cartooning. Launched against the advice of many who felt a "kid strip" wouldn't have a chance, *Dennis the Menace* very quickly achieved a circulation of hundreds of newspapers. A panel cartoon on weekdays, it becomes a comic strip on Sundays, drawn by one of Ketcham's assistants under the cartoonist's close supervision.

**92.** Johnny Hart (Born 1931), **B.C.** (February 17, 1958 - Present). August 10, 1975. Traces of blue pencil and graphite, half-tone film, pen and ink on bristol board, 11 × 16 in. (279 × 406 mm). Gift of the artist, The Ohio State University Cartoon Research Library. Copyright © 1975. Reprinted by permission of Johnny Hart and Creators Syndicate, Inc.

Inspired by Schulz's *Peanuts*, Hart was among the first of the succeeding generation of cartoonists to employ a similarly simple drawing style to regale readers with a different joke every day.

**93.** Tom K. Ryan (Born 1926), **Tumbleweeds** (September 1965 - Present). October 17, 1973. Traces of graphite, pen and ink on illustration board, 4 ¾ × 17 in. (121 × 432 mm). Collection of Mark J. Cohen and Rose Marie McDaniel. Copyright © 1973. Reprinted with special permission of King Features Syndicate.

*Tumbleweeds* is another of the modern breed of comic strip in which the humor arises from a dichotomy—in this case, between the mythology of the Old West and its reality. In the Hollywood myth, judges are fair and impartial and therefore have no ego; in Ryan's strip, the judge is all ego and self-interest.

strips were immediately singled out. Why would people read a story strip that takes two or three months to tell its tale when they can see an entire adventure in a hour on television? Editors stopped buying story strips; syndicates stopped buying them. They all bought gag strips instead (conveniently ignoring the fact that you can get more laughs in a half hour watching television than you are likely to get in the ten minutes it takes to read the funnies every day). Thus, gag strips were the de facto beneficiaries of the television age, inheriting the newspaper space once occupied by epic continuities. It was the immense success of *Beetle Bailey* and *Peanuts* that showed cartoonists how to survive the advent of television. At the same time, the arrival of these strips in the fall of 1950 signaled the beginning of the end for story strips. But no one realized it at the time. As we've observed, these new strips slipped into public view virtually unheralded.

A successful magazine cartoonist, Mort Walker imported to the funnies pages of American newspapers the simpler, less fustian, style of the magazine medium, helping (with Schulz) to set the pace for a generation of comic strip cartoonists. The title character in *Beetle Bailey* first appeared in *Saturday Evening Post* cartoons as a teenager named "Spider," but when the strip debuted, Spider had acquired a different insect monicker and was in college. The machinations of a lazy collegian, however, did not attract much attention just then: most American males were more likely to be drafted into the Korean War than to matriculate on college campuses. Walker cannily fell into step with his countrymen and put a uniform on Beetle in March 1951. The strip immediately picked up 100 new newspapers and grew steadily in circulation, eventually hitting 1,000—a mark that, until then, only *Blondie* had struck. (Ultimately, *Beetle Bailey* would pass 1,600; while *Blondie* and *Peanuts* passed 2,500.)

Even when the Korean hostilities ceased, Walker kept the military locale: the Selective Service made certain that every American male would sympathize with Beetle's predicaments. And by the time the draft

( CONTINUED PAGE 123 )

**94.** Russell Myers (Born 1938), **Broom-Hilda** (April 20, 1970 - Present). October 20, 1974. Traces of graphite, white gouache, pen and ink on illustration board, 12 ¼ × 27 ½ in. (311 × 699 mm). Philip Sills Collection, The Ohio State University Cartoon Research Library. Copyright © 1974 Tribune Media Services. All rights reserved. Reprinted with permission.

Myers' 1,500-year-old eponymous witch makes no appearance in the example at hand, but the cartoonist's inventive style is well displayed in this episode about Gaylord, Broom-Hilda's buzzard buddy. Myer's treatment of background and format is highly decorative and frequently quite fanciful, evoking memories of George Herriman's *Krazy Kat.* Here, the gag acquires at least some of its comedic impact from the use of narrow vertical panels that show action and inaction simultaneously.

**95.** Dik Browne (1917-1989), **Hagar the Horrible** (February 4, 1973 - Present). September 3, 1975. Pen, brush, and ink on illustration board, 3 1/2 × 11 3/8 in. (89 × 289 mm). Philip Sills Collection, The Ohio State University Cartoon Research Library.Copyright©1975. Reprinted with special permission of King Features Syndicate.

A champion of the daily joke, Browne joined Mort Walker in 1954 to help him do *Hi and Lois*, a domestic setting strip that Walker launched while also producing *Beetle Bailey*. In 1973, Browne added his own creation to his workload. Hagar is a childlike Viking chief and carouser, and the humor in the strip is character-driven and often anachronistic.

ended, the strip was not just about the Army. It had long before assumed a much more universal dimension: *Beetle Bailey* is a metaphor of all human society, the essential order of which is sustained through a hierarchy of authority which those in the society tend to see as ridden with incompetence. And since the downtrodden Private Bailey is as incompetent as General Halftrack or Sergeant Snorkle, the strip is a great leveler: we are equal because we all have frailties. Walker's drawing style had also evolved, becoming increasingly abstract until the pictures, too, were metaphorical, geometrically surreal representations of the humans whose antics they recorded (FIGURE 90).

Charles Schulz, meanwhile, was setting an entirely new fashion in both drawing style and humor. At first, he achieved his unique comedy by balancing the juvenile appearance of his characters against the adult cant they often uttered, the humor stemming from the contrast between the speakers and what they said. Eventually, once Charlie Brown's beagle Snoopy assumed a nearly human personality (he was tired of being a dog) and began imagining himself in World War I aerial battles with the Red Baron (in 1965) or writing novels, Schulz would juggle fantasy and reality to get laughs, alternating between the world atop the doghouse and the classroom or baseball diamond where the kids lived (FIGURES 87-88).

Arguably the world's most influential comic strip, *Peanuts* helped to set the modern fashion for the way a newspaper comic strip should be drawn. Schulz, like Walker, had been a magazine cartoonist and drew in a simpler manner than most newspaper cartoonists of the day. By the time *Peanuts* began soaring in circulation in the late 1950s, Schulz had refined his style even more, producing drawings that were starkly simple compared to the prevailing mode on the comics page—the style of Frank King or Chic Young

**96.** Jerry Dumas (Born 1930), **Sam's Strip** (October 1961-June 1963). June 16, 1962. Traces of graphite, pen and ink on illustration board, 4 1/2 x 16 in. (114 x 406 mm). Collection of Mark J. Cohen and Rose Marie McDaniel. Copyright © 1962. Reprinted with special permission of King Features Syndicate.

A strip unabashedly directed at comic strip buffs, *Sam's Strip* by Dumas and Mort Walker spoofed comic strips and the conventions thereof. Although it proved a little too rarified for general circulation, its characters returned in 1977 as the stars of a strip about small town policemen, *Sam and Silo*.

or Gladys Parker or Al Capp. Other new cartoonists who sought similar success copied the simplicity of Schulz's style. And sometimes they hadn't his skill, and their imitations were crude; but by then, newspaper editors, confronted by the success of some of Schulz's more skillful imitators, had been convinced that drawing ability didn't matter, and they bought the imitations, no matter how clumsy. Given the immense popularity and influence of the strip and its characters, and the pervasiveness of the licensed *Peanuts* paraphernalia, the second half of the first American comics century could well be dubbed the Age of Schulz.

The emergence of a simple drawing style as the prevailing manner for rendering gag-a-day strips was aided and abetted by another, much more insidious development in newspapering than the success of *Peanuts* and *Beetle Bailey*: newsprint shortages. This phenomenon was first felt in the funnies during World War II when newsprint supplies were strictly rationed so that sufficient wood pulp would be available for military use in manufacturing munitions. In order to cram more content into a limited number of pages, most newspapers reduced the amount of space allotted to comic strips. They didn't reduce the number of comic strips; they reduced the size of the strips. Comic strips routinely ran five columns wide before the war—10 1/4 x 3 inches. During the war, strips were only four columns wide, roughly 7 1/2 x 2 1/2 inches. Some newspapers ran some strips at their former width, but where that happened, the strips were cropped at the bottom by as much as twenty-five percent; so although they were still as wide as before, they were much shallower. Cartoonists were advised not to put any essential information at the bottom quarter of their strips' panels, and they complied without complaint: they were doing their patriotic duty. There was a war on. But once the war was over, they found that what they'd tolerated as a temporary condition had become

**97.** Jim Davis (Born 1945), **Garfield** (June 19, 1978 - Present). November 7, 1980. Blue pencil, applied half-tone, pen and ink on illustration board, 4 × 14 in. (102 × 356 mm). Jim Borgman Collection, The Ohio State University Cartoon Research Library. GARFIELD copyright © 1980 PAWS, Inc. Reprinted with permission of Universal Press Syndicate. All rights reserved.

Appearing in over 2,500 newspapers worldwide, *Garfield*, a talking animal strip about an overweight self-centered pet cat, is one of the three most widely circulated comic strips in history. In an age in which comic strip humor too often consists entirely of verbal witticisms, Davis successfully sustains a potent visual element in his comedy—as in this strip, in which the joke does not exist at all without the picture in the last panel. And the picture makes no sense without the verbal build-up of the two preceding panels. The inscription in water-smeared red is to cartoonist Jim Borgman.

permanent: most newspapers continued to publish comic strips at the reduced size. No one had complained yet, so why not? And editors, always jealous of the space they devoted to feature material, would have more space for news stories.

The Sunday funnies suffered as well. Newspapers, again seeking to make the most of their straitened circumstances during the war and desperate to retain advertising revenue despite the reduction in number of pages per issue, began selling space in the Sunday comics section to advertisers. And strips that had enjoyed full-page display before the war were cut back to half-page size; strips that had been published as half-page features were reduced to third-page size. And this practice continued after the war.

Newsprint was never available again at the rates newspapers had enjoyed before the war. There was, in effect, a perpetual shortage of newsprint. Over the years, newspapers surmounted this difficulty by slowly reducing their page size, thereby cutting down on the amount of newsprint needed every day. As the width of the page shrank, so did the width of comic strips. Comic strips were still published at the wartime half-page width, but a half-page by the 1990s was only three columns wide, not four. The average comic strip by then measured 6 x 1¾ inches. Serious storytelling strips felt the pinch more than gag-a-day strips. In such small panels, it was difficult to draw enough picture to produce the illusion of reality essential to making such narratives convincing and engrossing—particularly in adventure strips where exotic locale always had enhanced the action. Without space in which to illustrate, the visual rhetoric of the medium was seriously impaired. The adventure strip disappeared in the 1980s, the last serious attempt to sustain the genre being an offshoot of George Lucas' hugely popular movie series *Star Wars* (FIGURE 86). What remained of

( CONTINUED PAGE 128 )

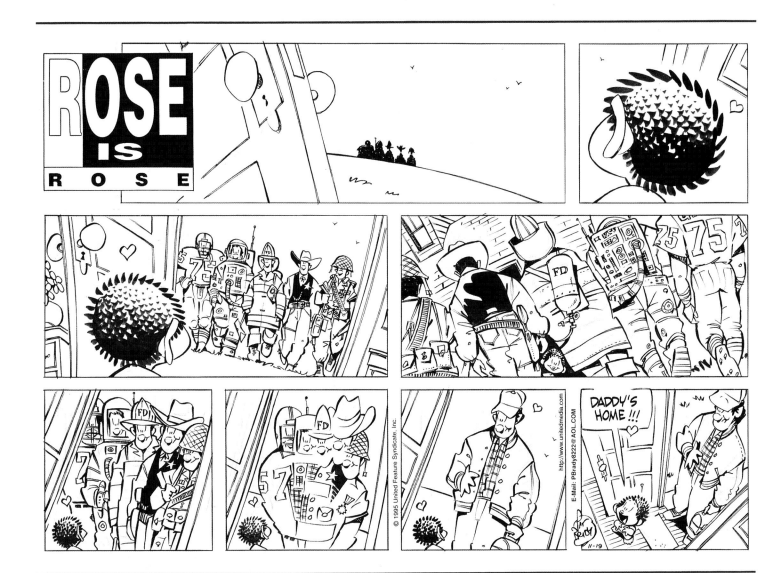

**98.** Pat Brady (Born 1947), **Rose Is Rose** (April 16, 1984 - Present). November 19, 1995. Blue pencil, pasteover, brush, pen and ink on illustration board, 13 5/8 × 19 1/2 in. (346 × 495 mm). Courtesy of the artist. Copyright © 1995. ROSE IS ROSE reprinted by permission of United Feature Syndicate, Inc.

Brady explores the potential of the medium in his strip more than most cartoonists do. He varies perspective wildly, the angle often creating the humor. His first panels are frequently visual puzzles, and their solution (sometimes a verbal "explanation," sometimes a reorientated point of view) constitutes the day's joke—as in the example at hand. But *Rose Is Rose* is more than clever visuals; it's also about domestic love and respect, and Brady creates this ambiance with a sure but never cloying hand. The light blue pencil preliminary sketching does not photograph in the engraving process.

**99.** Bill Holbrook (Born 1958), **On the Fastrack** (March 1984-Present). April 2, 1997. Pen and ink on tracing paper, laid down on illustration board, 3 1/4 × 12 7/8 in. (83 × 327 mm). Courtesy of the artist. Copyright © 1997. Reprinted with special permission of King Features Syndicate.

Although Holbrook's strip focuses on modern office life, the focus frequently shifts to the family life of a couple of the workers, whose domestic environment is as dominated by the computer as their work environment. Here, their two children struggle with the home computer. Extremely prolific, Holbrook also produces two other comic strips, *Safe Havens* (about preschoolers; begun in 1988) and *Kevin & Kell* (a talking animal strip available exclusively on the Internet, begun in 1995).

**100.** Bill Holbrook (Born 1958), **On the Fastrack** (March 1984-Present). January 20, 1998. Pen and ink on tracing paper, laid down on illustration board, 3 1/4 × 13 in. (83 × 330 mm). Courtesy of the artist. Copyright © 1998. Reprinted with special permission of King Features Syndicate.

Holbrook often makes adroit use of his medium, exploiting, particularly, its visual capacities. Here, the transformation of the character Art into a fox guarding the hen house in the last panel tells us all we need to know about how suited Art is to the task he has just been assigned.

To Phil Frank with best wishes ~ BILL WATTERSON

WITH THESE SNORKELS, WE CAN STAY UNDER WATER INDEFINITELY.

JUST THINK OF ALL THE FISH WE'LL BE ABLE TO SEE!

WE CAN COLLECT SHELLS! LET'S GO!

WELL SO FAR, THIS HAS BEEN A MAJOR DISAPPOINTMENT.

**101.** Bill Watterson (Born 1958), **Calvin and Hobbes** (November 1985 - December 31, 1995). August 16, 1986. Traces of graphite, white gouache, marker pen, brush, pen and ink on illustration board, 3 1/2 × 12 in. (95 × 305 mm). Collection of Phil Frank. CALVIN AND HOBBES copyright © 1986 Watterson.

A kid strip with a difference, the ostensible gimmick here is that the toy tiger, Hobbes, appears to his young owner as a real "person" but only when they are alone together; otherwise, Hobbes is just a stuffed animal. But the source of the strip's great appeal lies in the relationship between the boy and his tiger, their friendship, while

the basis of the humor in the strip is the personality of Calvin. Calvin is not just a mischievous little kid: he's the kind of kid Watterson himself would be if he could deploy his creative adult abilities to achieve juvenile ends. Watterson shocked his readers by retiring his award-winning strip after just a ten-year run, setting, perhaps, a precedent that other cartoonists will follow in the future. Two, indeed, already have: Berkeley Breathed (*Bloom County* and *Outland*) and Gary Larson (*The Far Side*). Watterson apparently lettered with a felt-tip pen, which uses an ink that fades to brown with age.

the continuity strip, the long-running soap opera strips, became talking-head strips: most of the space in every panel was devoted to rendering faces and filling speech balloons.

Gag-a-day strips, however, survived. And the simplified rendering style that surfaced in the post-war decade played right into the hands that fate was dealing: simply drawn strips could be reduced to the new small dimension with virtually no sacrifice of visual impact. And then, in an ironic twist, the simple drawing style could be used to justify the diminutive dimension of strips drawn in that fashion: editors looking at the minimalist artwork could find it easy to deny such strips any more than the barest minimum of display space. For such simple pictures, no more display space was needed. Thus, an accident of newspapering economy had unwittingly conspired with a trend in drawing style to ensure the triumph of the genre of strip typically rendered in that style. And with that, comics as a medium were consigned to minuscule display space, a condemnation that guaranteed, in effect, that the illustrative grandeur of the past would never again rise to demand more space in the newspaper editor's valuable news pages. And then the final irony: as newspapers sought in the 1980s to compete with television by increasing the visuals on their pages, they simultaneously ignored—even inhibited—the visual attraction of a medium native to those pages, the comic strip. In this environment, a strip with the visual complexity of Frank Cho's *Liberty Meadows* is a rarity. An accomplished and inventive cartoonist, Cho created an amazing hybrid—a comic strip that

**102.** Steve Bentley (Born 1954), **Herb and Jamaal** (August 7, 1989 - Present). August 16, 1993. Blue pencil, applied half-tone film, pen and ink on paper, 4¼ × 13½ in. (108 × 343 mm). Collection of Mark J. Cohen and Rose Marie McDaniel. Copyright © 1993 Tribune Media Services. All rights reserved. Reprinted with permission.

Bentley emphasizes relationships in his strip—the family relationships of Herb, and the ice cream store partnership of Herb and Jamaal. But the cartoonist also feels an obligation to portray the black experience in an authentic yet positive manner, so he often gets his characters involved in such street activities as the neighborhood watch, which brings up the subject of theft and gang activity but does it in an affirmative way.

displays his antic sense of humor in both simplified animation style and nearly realistic renderings, the former for manic animals, the latter for their human caregivers in an animal shelter (FIGURES 106-107).

Even at the reduced dimension, however, the comic strip medium retained astonishing vitality. Generation after generation of cartoonists continued to produce features in all the historic genres (except adventure and soap opera)—family strips, kid strips, animal strips. Some of the new strips featured racial minorities and other underrepresented groups—working mothers, single parents, and so on. And comic strips continued to demonstrate their enormous appeal. One of the animal strips, Jim Davis's *Garfield,* which celebrated the domestic cat as the epitome of laziness and self-absorption, nearly caught up to *Peanuts* in circulation by 1987, before the cat was ten years old (FIGURE 97). Scott Adams' *Dilbert* likewise became a phenomenon (FIGURE 123). By the mid-1990s, the title character was appearing regularly on the covers of newsstand magazines, demonstrating beyond quibble the ubiquitous popularity of the newspaper comic strip. Even as a newspaper character, Dilbert was so familiar and so popular a figure that other media could employ his image to attract readers.

The humor in the gag-a-day strips of the last decades of this century was increasingly sophisticated. The comic strip had become something more than mere entertainment. It had acquired a conscience. But the social role of comics had been underway since the 1930s, beginning in the midst of the Great Depression. ●

**103.** Rob Armstrong (Born 1962), **Jump Start** (October 2, 1989 - Present). October 4, 1993. Traces of blue pencil, applied half-tone film, white gouache, pen and ink on illustration board, 3⅜ × 11¾ in. (86 × 298 mm). Collection of Mark J. Cohen and Rose Marie McDaniel. Copyright © 1993. JUMP START reprinted by permission of United Feature Syndicate, Inc.

Although his strip's protagonists are African-American, Armstrong aims at creating a family strip about people who are persons, not members of a race. Still, this strip and others that feature black characters heighten the visibility of this significant portion of the American population.

## The Sophistication of the Modern Gag Strip

The initial success of *Peanuts* had its roots in the humorous contrast between what we saw (little kids) and what they seemed to be doing and saying (which reflected much more adult concerns). Humor arising from this kind of dichotomy, "non-sequitur humor," is another aspect of *Peanuts* that set a comic strip fashion. Or, if it did not exactly set the fashion (a debatable point since the "sick jokes" and "elephant jokes" of the fifties turn on a similar comic device), it was at least the first strip to capture and capitalize on a mode of humorous thinking then "in the air." Two other new strips that have at their core some adaptation of the principles of non-sequitur humor are *B.C.* and *Tumbleweeds.* In each strip, as in *Peanuts,* the adaptation is original, inventive, and highly individual. In each strip, the reader finds again the devices and techniques made familiar to him in *Peanuts*—deceptively simple artwork, personality traits sharpened nearly to the point of eccentricity, repetition of set pieces, the running gag, animals with human aspirations.

Another of the new breed of comic strip cartoonists who apprenticed in magazine cartooning, Johnny Hart started *B.C.* on February 17, 1958. Inspired by what he saw in *Peanuts,* he drew in a simple, magazine cartoon style, and his strip, like Schulz's, depended for its humorous impact upon a dichotomy between what the reader saw and

what the characters said. The setting for *B.C.* is prehistoric; but the concerns and preoccupations of its characters are entirely contemporary. Hence, even in this unlikely setting, we were delightfully surprised to discover—ourselves. But with a difference. Man, as always, is the inventor, the discoverer. And there is a childlike (and therefore entirely human) delight in discovery, invention—in other words, in novelty. But an invention lands in the world of *B.C.* full-blown, without having evolved from a need. Like children, the prehistoric characters in *B.C.* fasten on some new device without fully understanding its function or the principles upon which its operation rests. Newly discovered devices are not put to their proper use: they remain novelties, oddities, things that fit into our world, but not quite into theirs. Thor's invention of the wheel is a prize specimen. The wheel of which Thor is so proud isn't attached to a vehicle: it's just a circular stone that he rides by straddling as if it were a horse. *B.C.* evolved into something else over the years, and its humor eventually depended less and less upon anachronism; still, it has a sophistication that only a strip in the Age of Schulz could support (FIGURE 92).

*Tumbleweeds* is another of the same modern breed. Launching his strip in September 1965, Tom K. Ryan built up the ideal of the Old West and then punched holes in it. The discrepancy or dichotomy is

# FoxTrot
## BILL AMEND

**104.** Bill Amend (Born 1962), **FoxTrot** (April 10, 1988 - Present). September 14, 1997. Traces of graphite, marker pen, pen and ink on bristol board, 9 1/8 × 13 in. (232 × 330 mm). Courtesy of the artist. FOXTROT copyright © 1997 Bill Amend. Reprinted with permission of Universal Press Syndicate. All rights reserved.

The family strip is a permanent fixture on most comics pages, and Amend's effort joins a distinguished roster. But *FoxTrot* is different from others of its genre: the strip consistently presents family life from the point of view of the children, not the parents. And in this example, that difference is dramatized: the action itself is depicted through the eyes of Peter, the teenage son. We see only what he sees, and these views become a sort of puzzle which is explained by the last panel. Our surprise at the explanation prompts a laugh of satisfaction. Amend deliberately chose a vaguely cubist manner of drawing to emphasize the modernity of his family.

between the myth of the Old West and its reality. Ryan's diminutive characters set the stage with their cuteness: they are so cute that we expect to encounter here a child's rosy version of the Old West. Ryan inflates the speech of his characters to match the yearnings that the pictures seem to express, but the facts of life deflate this scenario. The dialogue abounds in the clichés and doggerel mythology of the dime-novel Western, but reality is seldom as highflown as the prose. The title character's steed is not the noble cliché of yesterday's Roy Rogers movie: he's a moth-eaten army surplus cayuse, and he can never quite live up to the expectations of his master who celebrates in his mind's eye the wild and wooly West of Hollywood, not historical fact. The cowboy hero Tumbleweeds, despite his aspirations, must live in this world, not in his dreams. On every hand, assumptions built on the Old West of motion picture and legend are disappointed. The sheriff can capture the town hoodlum, but can't lock him up in jail; the judge is blind to justice; the heroine is not a modestly blushing shy young desert blossom—she's painfully plain and aggressively desperate to catch a man. Not even the Indians live up to the Hollywood sterotype: hardly savages, they must go to school and take evening classes in the theory and practice of bloodthirsty warfare.

Even if our fond anticipations are destined to be blighted, the lesson of the strip is not bleak. Tumbleweeds' dreams may be doomed

**105.** Patrick McDonnell (Born 1956), **Mutts** (September 5, 1994 - Present). November 3, 1996. Traces of graphite, white gouache, pen and ink on paper, 5¼ × 16 in. (133 × 406 mm). Courtesy of the artist. Copyright © 1996. Reprinted with special permission of King Features Syndicate.

A biographer of George Herriman, McDonnell admires the spirit of the immortal *Krazy Kat,* and *Mutts* has some of that flavor about it—warm-hearted epiphanies, and momentary humane revelations. Although McDonnell's animals talk, they talk only to each other—and only when none of the strip's human characters are around. They think and behave like pets, not humans in the shape of animals.

---

to disappointment, but there is no bitter disillusionment here—only a remarkable resilience. The characters turn quickly from their fancies to the facts and embrace reality. Hildegarde wants Tumbleweeds as her husband, but, in the last analysis, any man will do. The realities do not crush these pint-sized dreamers; nor do they quite wake them up (FIGURE 93).

The humor in these new strips is more sophisticated than comic strip comedy had been in the past. The humor of *Blondie* was, and is, humor appropriate to the setting in which the characters are developed and appropriate to the characters themselves. The success of the punchline does not rest on our ability to recognize a dichotomy or discrepancy between characters and setting, dialogue and action. The humor of *Bugs Bunny* or of *Donald Duck* does not originate in their being animals behaving like humans as it does with Snoopy in *Peanuts.* Nor, in these two strips, does the comedy come from the animals behaving like animals as it sometimes does in *Pogo* or in *Animal Crackers.* The humor in the strips of this new tradition—*Pogo, Peanuts, B.C., The Wizard of Id, Tumbleweeds, Animal Crackers,* to name a few—is more sophisticated because it depends on our recog-

nizing something that is only implicit in the strip. We laugh at *B.C.* because we are shown childlike men, men just beginning to be men, trying out civilization, and we see what they do not: like a suit that's too large, civilization doesn't quite fit. We laugh at *Tumbleweeds* much of the time because we recognize that the real Old West was quite different from the West that the diminutive Tumbleweeds tries to reenact. If we didn't know that the best use of wheels is to support and facilitate the movement of carts or vehicles, Thor's wheel wouldn't appear funny to us at all. If we didn't know that most cowboys' horses don't jump wide chasms in a single bound, Tumbleweeds' dashed hopes would be tragic instead of comic. But we do know these things, and upon that knowledge the humor of these strips is built.

The humor of dichotomy—because it points to a discrepancy, a non-sequitur—is inevitably sobering. In *Tumbleweeds,* for example, it isn't just the Old West that the characters try to create with their language, and it isn't just the Old West that can't live up to its poetry. Man hovers between the lines here, and he is a bit short of his vision of himself too. Just as he is in *B.C.* and in *Pogo.*

**106.** Frank Cho (Born 1971), **Liberty Meadows** (March 31, 1997-Present). February 2, 1998. Traces of graphite, pen and ink on bristol board, 4 3/4 × 16 in. (121 × 406 mm). Courtesy of the artist. Copyright © 1998. Reprinted by permission of Frank Cho and Creators Syndicate, Inc.

The cast of *Liberty Meadows* resides at an animal sanctuary of that name and includes talking animals as well as administering humans. In the animal ranks are Ralph, a midget circus bear; Leslie, a giant frog; and Dean, a male chauvinist pig (and former fraternity mascot), who appears here with the beauteous Brandy, the female human

who is the animal psychologist. Dean is at Liberty Meadows to be de-toxified, but, as we see, he resists all attempts to cure him of his smoking habit. Cho's command of the capacities of the strip medium are impressive. Here, he embraces Dean's crucial activity in a single panel frame, the repetition of Dean's figure within which gives the strip a visual impact on the comics page different from that of its fellows—and it also focuses the reader's attention on Dean. The first and last panels "bookend" the central action with nice symmetry.

**107.** Frank Cho (Born 1971), **Liberty Meadows** (March 31, 1997 - Present). August 10, 1997. Traces of graphite, white gouache, pen and ink on bristol board, 7 7/8 × 23 3/4 in. (200 × 603 mm). Courtesy of the artist. Copyright © 1997. Reprinted by permission of Frank Cho and Creators Syndicate, Inc.

Cho often parodies other strips or aspects of popular culture in his Sunday strips. Here, in a parody of Hal Foster's famed *Prince Valiant*, he displays his superb

drawing ability, the likes of which we seldom see on the comics pages at the end of the medium's first century. In the course of his spoof, Cho takes a jab at newspapers for allotting so little space to comic strips, a visual art form that requires more space to be effective; and he also jokes self-consciously about the comics by portraying Ralph and Leslie as "readers" (or as characters?) finding their way through the funnies section.

JIM— THIS COULD EVEN BE MORE CASUAL IF YOU THINK IT WOULD WORK BETTER — MEANING JEREMY COULD JUST BE WALKING BY AND JUMP WITHOUT COILING FIRST. (?)

**108A.** Jerry Scott (Born 1956), story sketch for **Zits.** 1997. Pen and ink on paper. Courtesy of Jim Borgman. Copyright © 1997. Reprinted with special permission of King Features Syndicate.

**108B.** Jim Borgman (Born 1954) and Jerry Scott (Born 1956), **Zits** (July 1997-Present). August 8, 1997. Traces of graphite, pen and ink on illustration board. 4 ⁵/₈ × 14 ¹/₄ in. (117 × 362 mm). Courtesy of Jim Borgman. Copyright © 1997. Reprinted with special permission of King Features Syndicate.

A recent entry into the lists of teenage strips, *Zits* pokes fun at teenagers and at their parents. Ostensibly drawn by Borgman and written by Scott, the strip's daily installments have an unusual gestation: Scott, who is a cartoonist himself, submits his "script" to Borgman in the form of a rough sketch of the strip (top); then Borgman produces the final art (bottom). Borgman sometimes modifies Scott's idea: in the example at hand, Borgman clearly felt that Jeremy's father was the more appropriate candidate for climbing a ladder. This example, like several of the Borgman-Scott productions, exploits the nature of the medium: seeing Jeremy leap out of the panel of the strip (that is, out of sight) in the third panel, we wonder what could explain his behavior. The explanation supplies the day's gag.

# Comics With a Conscience: Satire and Social Commentary

## MOVEMENT 5

SATIRE IS THE USUAL SIGNAL of status for comics. If a comic strip is satirical, then it has a social conscience and seriousness of purpose and, therefore, cultural status above mere entertainment. This is a remnant of our Puritan heritage: nothing is worthwhile unless it has seriousness of purpose. We have broadened our view considerably since the days of Cotton Mather: today entertainers enjoy a social standing above that of politicians. But for the first part of the first century of comics, comics were mostly for entertainment, and entertainment was not regarded as essential to the otherwise serious (puritanical) purposes of society. By the middle of the century, however, comics had acquired a satirical edge, and their social conscience was on display.

Satire has always been the province of cartoonists. Their humor is inherently satirical. Indeed, much ordinary, day-to-day humor is satirical if we employ the usual dictionary definition of satire: "A literary (or other) work in which irony, derision, or wit in any form is used to expose folly or wickedness." Thus, when a cartoonist depicts the antics or preoccupations of a fellow member of the human race in order to show how foolish those endeavors are, he is a satirist. The product of his effort in this instance is social satire: it ridicules homo sapiens generally—as a species or as a social creature—launching many a penetrating sidelong glance askance at the often silly conventions of society itself. Social satire induces us to laugh at ourselves. Political satire, on the other hand, aims at specific targets—malefactors and fools in public office, government policy gone awry, unfair labor practices, bullying unions, and so on. Political satire aims at getting us to act as well as to laugh (and when we laugh, it is not at ourselves).

Thomas Nast remains the emblem of political satire in the early days. Nast's cartoons ridiculing and exposing Boss Tweed in New York in the 1870s effectively drove the politician out of power. (Tweed fled the country, and when he was finally arrested in Spain, it was because the authorities recognized him

(CONTINUED PAGE 138)

see page 138: **109.** Harold Gray, **Little Orphan Annie**

**109.** Harold Gray (1894-1968), **Little Orphan Annie** (August 5, 1924- Present). September 22, 1936. Traces of graphite, pen and ink on illustration board, 5 1/2 x 19 3/4 in. (140 x 502 mm). Collection of Robert Stolzer. Copyright © 1936 Tribune Media Services. All rights reserved. Reprinted with permission.

Casting his orphan teenager adrift in the wilds of Depression-ridden America, Gray ensured her survival by making her supremely self-reliant. Gray's graphic and narrative style often shrouded the proceedings in a cloak of menace, and the characters were always looking furtively over their shoulders.

from Nast's pictures.) Cartoonists working the weekly humor magazines of the late nineteenth century deployed political as well as social satire. And so did newspaper cartoonists in those formative years.

To unfurl another of those overlapped developments that our survey passed over earlier, let us return to Bud Fisher's *Mutt and Jeff.* The strip was born in 1907 as social satire: it ridiculed the obsessions of gamblers. But Fisher also ventured into political satire. In a trial staged in the strip during February and March 1908, Fisher depicted the prosecuting attorney and the various minions of the law surrounding him in ways that would remind his readers of several local politicians who were recently implicated in a case of corruption in the city government of San Francisco. And Fisher probably was not the only newspaper cartoonist plunging his pen into such local political brouhahas in those days. Even Outcault's Yellow Kid made comments on political matters from time to time. But once comic strips became syndicated for national distribution, this kind of specific political target was abandoned. A national readership wouldn't be interested in the shenanigans of New York City's politicians or San Francisco's. If cartoonists were to take up political matters, those matters would necessarily have to be national in scope. But that was too risky.

Syndicated cartoonists eschewed taking political potshots in their strips because the objective of syndication was to attain publication in papers in every hamlet in the land, and the odds of reaching this goal weren't very good if the comics expressed political views with which the local editors might disagree. Hence, "pure" entertainment became the coin of the syndicated comic strip realm—with the result that comics were often seen by the mavens of culture as somewhat frivolous. Not that politics were altogether forbidden. Fisher often ran his characters for United States president during election years (beginning in 1908), but he spoofed politics generally rather than the views of one candidate or another. And Sidney Smith did the same

**110.** Al Capp (1909-1979), **Li'l Abner** (August 13, 1934-November 13, 1977). April 25, 1936. Traces of graphite, pen and ink on illustration board, 5 3/8 × 22 3/8 in. (137 × 572 mm). Collection of the Cartoon Art Museum, San Francisco. Copyright © Capp Enterprises, Inc. Reprinted with permission of Capp Enterprises, Inc. All rights reserved.

At the core of Capp's satire was the contrast between the Yokum family (Li'l Abner, Mammy, and Pappy) and all civilized society outside the hills of Dogpatch. The innocence of the former revealed the corruption of the latter—and vice versa. Here, beginning in the second panel, we see L'il Abner's double, Gat Garson, an out-and-out criminal who appeared in the strip from time to time, his evil personality suggesting that even L'il Abner—if raised in society rather than Dogpatch—would have been corrupted.

in 1922 when he ran Andy Gump for Congress. And that's pretty much how matters stood until Harold Gray ran up against Franklin D. Roosevelt in the 1930s.

Gray is celebrated these days as an arch conservative who openly voiced his political opinions in his strip *Little Orphan Annie* (FIGURE 109). While Gray was clearly a conservative, he didn't impose his views on his characters from outside; rather, those views were organic, growing naturally out of the very concept of the strip. The best way for a little orphan girl to make her way in the world without being simply a weepy milksop was for her to be self-reliant. As a good storyteller, Gray knew that, and his characters and their attitudes were the logical extension of this central notion. At the end of the second month of the strip's run (September 1924), Gray introduced the character who would shape the philosophy of independence represented by the resourceful Annie into a political stance: Annie is adopted by Oliver "Daddy" Warbucks, a millionaire industrialist. Warbucks became Gray's example of the self-made man, the self-reliant individualist who made himself what he is through purposeful enterprise. The epitome of this American culture hero, Warbucks is the larger-than-life version of what all the "little people" in the strip inevitably become if they follow Annie's example of hard work and canny capitalism. Without knowing it at the time, Gray had started his strip along a collision course. And by 1932, he reached the fated destination.

Elected in 1932 to save the country from the Great Depression, Franklin Delano Roosevelt rose to the challenge by assuming that government was responsible for the welfare of its people. Under FDR's tutelage, the downtrodden and the poor were encouraged to look to government for help rather than exhorted to help themselves by working hard and exercising diligently the principles of free enterprise. Gray's message was precisely the opposite. As Gray's exemplar, Warbucks could scarcely espouse self-reliance and free

**111.** Al Capp (1909-1979), **Li'l Abner** (August 13, 1934-November 13, 1977). September 1, 1957. Blue pencil, white gouache, pen and ink on illustration board, 18 × 27½ in. (457 × 699 mm). Collection of Frank Pauer. Copyright © Capp Enterprises, Inc. Reprinted with permission of Capp Enterprises, Inc. All rights reserved.

Capp regularly parodied other comic strips in *Li'l Abner*. Practiced at seeing through the pretenses of the social order, Capp could easily detect the fallacies that formed the foundation of such social institutions as the soap opera comic strip *Mary Worth*. Capp's parody of the strip suggested that if there ever existed such a kindly little old neighbor lady as the strip's title character, her attempts at helping others would be more likely to destroy their lives than improve them. Mary Worm is a meddler, not an enabler, and not even her son welcomes her ministrations. His appearance here completes the parody: *Mary Worth* was written by Allen Saunders.

**112.** Al Capp (1909-1979), **Li'l Abner** (August 13, 1934 - November 13, 1977). October 27, 1964. Blue pencil, white gouache, pen and ink on illustration board, 5½ x 18¾ in. (140 x 476 mm). Charles H. Kuhn Collection, The Ohio State Cartoon Research Library. Copyright © Capp Enterprises, Inc. Reprinted with permission of Capp Enterprises, Inc. All rights reserved.

Capp so frequently spoofed Chester Gould's *Dick Tracy* that the parody character, Fearless Fosdick, became a regular member of the cast in *Li'l Abner.* Gould, who took his law-and-order mission pretty seriously, nonetheless delighted in Capp's antics: he said he was the only cartoonist in the world who had a great comic strip artist for a press agent—absolutely free.

enterprise during the Roosevelt years without, at the same time, attacking Roosevelt's policies. And so *Little Orphan Annie* became the first nationally syndicated comic strip to be unabashedly, unrelievedly, "political." But it had acquired a political posture because the very essence of its story demanded it.

At just about the same time as "Daddy" Warbucks began his confrontation with the New Deal, another comic strip was launched that would edge the medium further into the arena of overt political satire. Al Capp's *Li'l Abner* began August 13, 1934, but it didn't begin as a political satire at all. At first, it was wholly social satire.

In the first sixteen months of his life, Li'l Abner, the quintessential hillbilly, spends more time in New York City than in the hills of his home in Dogpatch. And in that circumstance is the flywheel of the strip's satirical dynamic. At the very point of our meeting Li'l Abner, Mammy and Pappy Yokum, and the lovelorn Daisy Mae, Abner gets a letter from his rich Aunt Bessie, who invites him to spend time with her in New York society in order to acquire polish and to enjoy "the advantages of wealth and luxury." Abner goes to the big city and stays there for the next four months. The episodes in New York, where Abner encounters civilization, contrast his country simplicity against society's sophistication—or, more precisely, his innocence against its decadence, his purity against its corruption. The comedy arises from this clash of cultures: we laugh to see Abner's simpleminded struggle against the forces of civilization that seem to him so inexplicable, so utterly without practical foundation, and we roar with satisfaction when he eventually triumphs—his ignorance as intact as his innocence—over the twisted insincerity of "high society." One episode is virtually a metaphor for Capp's technique.

**113.** Walt Kelly (1913-1973), **Pogo** (May 16, 1949- July 20, 1975). May 13, 1953. Blue pencil, pen and ink on illustration board, 4 1/2 × 16 3/8 in. (114 × 416 mm). Pogo Collection, The Ohio State University Cartoon Research Library. Copyright © 1953 Walt Kelly Estate.

When Simple J. Malarkey resorts to outright intimidation (as here) to impose his will on others, Kelly's portrait of the senator from Wisconsin is complete, and Joseph McCarthy is exposed as a buccaneer and a bully, not a patriot. Kelly occasionally varied the style of lettering for speech balloons to imply something about the personality of the speaker; here, Old English type suggests the dignified, old fashioned, even prudish, character of Deacon Mushrat [sic].

**114.** Walt Kelly (1913-1973), **Pogo** (May 16, 1949- July 20, 1975). March 22, 1968. Blue pencil, pasteover, pen and ink on illustration board, 5 1/2 × 20 in. (140 × 508 mm). Pogo Collection, The Ohio State University Cartoon Research Library. Copyright © 1968 Walt Kelly Estate.

In the 1968 Presidential election season, Kelly deployed wind-up toys for many of the candidates, invoking the formula of a popular series of jokes then current. ("What happens when you wind up a politician?" "He runs for something.") The strip's perennial promoter of candidacies, the bear P.T. Bridgeport, speaks in the typography of circus posters, completing the allusion to a famous citizen of Kelly's adopted Connecticut hometown, P.T. Barnum, and proffering Kelly's opinion of political campaigns. The Nelson Rockefeller wind-up is forever seeking to appeal to everyone by his moderate stance, while the George Romney toy falls down, just as the candidate Romney did when he confessed to being brainwashed about Vietnam. Kelly made his preliminary sketches with a light-blue pencil (which does not photograph in the engraving process), and here the underlying drawing suggests that his initial conception of the design for Lyndon B. Johnson (who hadn't, yet, taken himself out of the race) had the long horn steer's horns more upright than horizontal.

**115.** Walt Kelly (1913-1973), **Pogo** (May 16, 1949-July 20, 1975). March 2, 1969. Blue pencil, pasteover, pen and ink on illustration board, 16 × 23 3/8 in. (406 × 594 mm). Pogo Collection, The Ohio State University Cartoon Research Library. Copyright © 1969 Walt Kelly Estate.

Kelly's Sunday pages were usually not satirical or topical. Instead, they were often highly fanciful, combining vaudevillian nonsense with snatches of fairy-tale lore. By the late 1960s, his artwork had become very detailed and ornate; trees and other flora lovingly embellished with curling tendrils and lacy feathering.

## Right-wing Capp?

In his last years, Capp was roundly criticized (by liberals) for the unyielding rigor of his attacks on the New Left. It was claimed that he had defected from the liberal camp and had gone over to the Right. But that was not so.

Capp's objectives remained the same as always. The fanaticism of the New Left was no less a human folly than the rigidity of the Right in seeking to preserve the conventions of its social order. Capp took folly where he found it (the more contemporary, the better) and unceremoniously ripped the self-righteous veils away. His method permitted no qualifying disclaimers, no equivocating; so his burlesque seemed narrow and single-minded. It was, however, just burlesque—the hardest-hitting kind of satire.

Despite the assault tactics of his method, Capp saw himself as affirming something, not as attacking something. The thing he affirmed was the opposite of everything he attacked. He told people that he was a propagandist for love.

**DOONESBURY**

*For Milton Caniff with great admiration from Garry Trudeau   8/6/71*

by Garry Trudeau

**116.** Garry Trudeau (Born 1948), **Doonesbury** (October 26, 1970 - Present). August 19, 1971. Pen and ink on illustration board, 4⅝ × 14½ in. (117 × 368 mm). Milton Caniff Collection, The Ohio State University Cartoon Research Library. DOONESBURY copyright © 1971 G.B. Trudeau. Reprinted with permission of Universal Press Syndicate. All rights reserved.

Embodying a counter culture point of view at first, Trudeau's strip assaulted not only the middle class but the political establishment, often taking unpopular but principled stands on national issues. Trudeau's satirical technique is outright assault, not veiled allegory: he names names when foraging in the political jungle, and he pulls no punches, declining to soften or mute an attack. Visually, he developed a static style, presenting the same picture panel after panel, the unrelenting repetition creating a unique inner tension for his narrative. The seeming emotionlessness of his characters as they confront inflammatory issues heightens the sense of injury that the illogic of the situation ought to inspire: why aren't they outraged? They evidently aren't, so we, the readers, must be.

A phony baron with an impressive beard (actually, a penniless confidence man) goes after Aunt Bessie's hand in marriage, his eye exclusively on her fortune. Abner finds out that the baron's intentions are less than honorable, but he's helpless to do anything about it. His first instinct is to "smack the baron aroun' somewhut an' throw him outa th' house," but he recognizes that this behavior isn't gentlemanly, and since his Mammy has sent him to Aunt Bessie to learn to be a gentleman, he dutifully refrains from taking this course of action. And when he decides simply to go to Aunt Bessie and tell her what a lout the baron is, he learns that his aunt is very happy because she believes herself in love. Rather than destroy her happiness, he says nothing to her about the mercenary intentions of her soon-to-be husband. It seems that Bessie is doomed to be duped. At the last moment—just before the wedding—Abner remembers a smattering of his Mammy's wisdom: "Anyone which is a skunk looks like one." Putting this axiom into practice, he gets a razor and forcibly gives the phony baron a shave. Without his imposing beard, the con-man is revealed as a nearly chinless simp. Bessie is no longer impressed, and she calls off the wedding.

Capp was well on the way to becoming a master satirist. Again and again over the next decades, Capp would perform this operation—stripping the pretensions away, revealing society (all civilization perhaps) as mostly artificial, often shallow and self-serving, usually greedy, and, ultimately, meaningless.

**117.** Garry Trudeau (Born 1948), **Doonesbury** (October 26, 1970-Present). May 30, 1990. Blue pencil, applied half-tone film, brush, pen and ink on illustration board, 4 1/2 × 14 3/4 in. (117 × 375 mm). Gift of the artist, The Ohio State University Cartoon Research Library. DOONESBURY copyright (c) 1990 G.B. Trudeau. Reprinted with permission of Universal Press Syndicate. All rights reserved.

Trudeau took on social issues as well as political ones. One of his characters dies of AIDS and makes a videotape to be played as his funeral service. In discussing the fatal illness openly, Trudeau helped remove the shrouding taboo, thereby making considera-tion of funding for research more likely. Here, the casual attitude of the dead man seems to ridicule our morbid fascination with the subject of death and the hereafter. Making the tape before his death, the character could scarcely know that the Muppet master Jim Henson is in heaven (or, even, if there is a heaven)—yet we are tricked into accepting the report on Henson's whereabouts based upon the seeming testimony of one who ought to know, a dead man. By this time in the strip's run, the distinctive static images have disappeared and the artwork was inked by an assistant, Don Carlton.

But this was social satire, not political satire. It was man and his society that comprised Capp's primary targets. As a satirist, he ridiculed the pretensions and foibles of humanity—avariciousness, bigotry, egocentricity, selfishness, vaulting ambition. All of man's baser instincts, which Capp saw manifest in many otherwise socially acceptable guises, were his targets. And he took as his task the unhorsing of the preten-sions that masked those follies. Li'l Abner was the perfect foil in this enterprise: naive and unpretentious (and, not to gloss over the matter, just plain stupid), he believed in all the idealistic preachments of his fellow man—and was therefore the ideal victim for their practices (which invariably fell far short of their noble utterances). In a sense, Abner was Capp's version of Rousseau's natural man. Destined to do battle with civilized man, Abner would be both champion and fall guy. Because most of us are idealists (in name, at least), we see in Abner an aspect of ourselves. But we also see his stupidity—and thus we see how stupid we are if we believe in what we say too uncritically, without realistic allowances and skeptical reappraisals (FIGURE 110).

We cannot, after all, escape the human condition. We can try, but only if we recognize it for what it is, if we undeceive ourselves about our most fondly held self-images, if we tear the rose-tinted spectacles from our eyes, can we hope to achieve any measure of success at being what we want to be. Capp

**118.** Cathy Guisewite (Born 1950), **Cathy** (November 22, 1976 - Present). June 18, 1984. Traces of white gouache, applied half-tone film, pen and ink on illustration board, 4 5/8 × 14 1/2 in. (117 × 368 mm). June 18, 1984. Gift of the Artist, The Ohio State University Cartoon Research Library. CATHY copyright © 1984 Cathy Guisewite. Reprinted with permission of Universal Press Syndicate. All rights reserved.

Originating in Guisewite's self-deprecating doodles in letters home, *Cathy* is the first comic strip to focus on what is supposedly a typical unmarried young career woman balancing the demands of her job against her aspirations for a better love life. The title character is expert in self-analysis, and the perspective Guisewite assumes is necessarily a wry one.

tried to help us accomplish this by showing us what we sometimes are and by contrasting that to what we say we are.

The politicization of Li'l Abner proceeded from the strip's fundamental equation. Capp's vehicle was Rabelaisian burlesque, a mode of satirical comment that allows no fine gray shadings—only stark blacks and naked whites. Painted only in those values, the world Capp showed us was inherently divided into neat compartments. The biggest divisions of all were the simplest—the Good (the eternal Yokums with the ever-lastingly shrewd Mammy guiding their footsteps) and the Bad (most of the rest of the world). But there were other divisions implicit in Capp's black-and-white portrait. Because he attacked the conventions of modern civilized society and because the most conspicuous upholders of those conventions were the wealthy and the powerful members of the establishment and because America's establishment was then (and is now) mostly political conservatives, most of the icons Capp smashed so jubilantly were the icons of the Right. And by extrapolating from this circumstance, Capp's readers assumed that the cartoonist was a liberal.

He wasn't. Or, if he was, he was still more satirist than political advocate. But his kind of satire paved the way to the next kind, the kind with a specific political target. And Walt Kelly was the first to take aim.

In Kelly's great *Pogo,* the comic strip achieved the maximum of which the medium is capable, a zenith of high art. If we accept the definition of comic strip art as a narrative of words and pictures, in which neither words nor pictures are quite satisfactory alone without the other, then we must say that Kelly welded the verbal and visual elements together into a comic chorus so unified, so mutually dependent, that it crystallized forever the very essence of the art.

**119.** Morrie Turner (Born 1923), **Wee Pals** (1964 - Present). April 3, 1986. Traces of graphite, pen and ink on Craftint board, 3½ × 13¼ in. (89 × 337 mm). Collection of Mark J. Cohen and Rose Marie McDaniel. Copyright © 1986. Reprinted by permission of Morrie Turner and Creators Syndicate, Inc.

The first African-American cartoonist to produce a nationally distributed comic strip raising racial consciousness, Turner has consistently promulgated a benevolent message of harmony as well as humor. Turner used Craftint board for gray tones, and with age, the Craftint fades to brown.

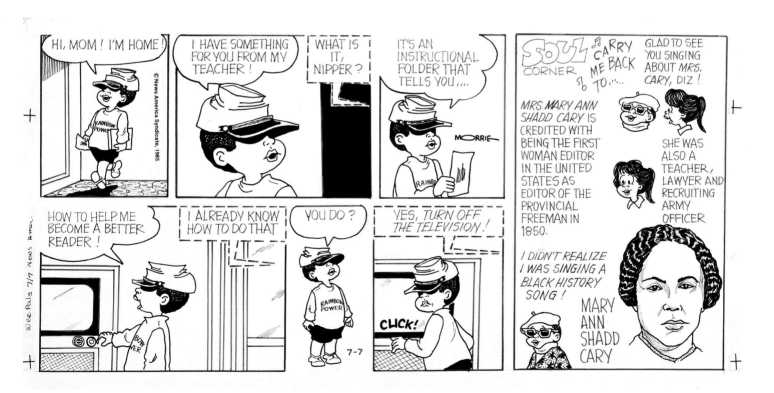

**120.** Morrie Turner (Born 1923), **Wee Pals** (1964 - Present). July 7, 1985. Traces of graphite, white gouache, pen and ink on illustration board, 10 × 21 in. (254 × 533 mm). Morrie Turner Collection, The Ohio State University Cartoon Research Library. Copyright © 1985. Reprinted by permission of Morrie Turner and Creators Syndicate, Inc.

Turner's gang of youngsters is so racially diverse that when they sought a name for their club, they chose "Rainbow Power Club."

**121.** Berke Breathed (Born 1957), **Bloom County** (December 8, 1980 - August 6, 1989). August 7, 1988. Blue pencil, pasteovers, red ink, pen and ink on illustration board, 13 1/2 × 19 3/8 in. (343 × 492 mm). Collection of Mark J. Cohen and Rose Marie McDaniel. Copyright (c) 1988, The Washington Post Writers Group. Reprinted with permission.

*Bloom County* may have benefitted shortly after its launch from the sabbatical that Garry Trudeau took (discontinuing *Doonesbury,* January 1983 - September 1984). Because Breathed's drawing style is reminiscent of Trudeau's and his sense of humor is often directed at political targets, many newspapers ran the strip in the place that Trudeau had left vacant. Also like Trudeau, Breathed won a Pulitzer Prize for editorial cartooning (a distinction among comic strip cartoonists that only Trudeau had achieved before him), but his pen doesn't drip as much vitriol as Trudeau's, and he aimed more often at social mores or popular culture than politics. Here, he gently ribs the colorless George Bush, using the winsome character that became so popular as to outlast the strip itself, Opus the penguin.

**122.** Ted Shearer (about 1939-about 1986), **Quincy** (June 17, 1971-about 1986). December 20, 1979. Traces of graphite, white gouache, applied half-tone film, marker, pen and ink on illustration board, 4 1/2 × 15 in. (114 × 381 mm). Collection of Mark J. Cohen and Rose Marie McDaniel. Copyright © 1979. Reprinted with special permission of King Features Syndicate.

One of the earliest comic strips to focus on the African-American experience in an inner city environment, Shearer's pioneering strip didn't preach: it simply showed with gentle humor what life was like for a ten-year-old boy in the city. A beautifully rendered strip, the street scenes against which Quincy played out his life always smacked of authenticity.

*Pogo* seemed to be just a funny animal strip set in a southern swamp, but in Kelly's hands, the strip reached beyond its tradition. At its core, Kelly's creation was a reincarnation of vaudeville, its routines often laced with humor that derived from pure slapstick. To that, Kelly added the remarkably fanciful and inventive language of his characters—a "southern fried" dialect that lent itself readily to his characters' propensity to take things literally, and permitted a shameless delight in puns. All this was funny enough, but in 1952, three years after national syndication of the strip began, Kelly ran Pogo for President of the United States (against Dwight Eisenhower and Adlai Stevenson). Pogo lost (as you may have noticed), but the popularity of his campaign showed Kelly that the time was ripe to enter a whole new field of comedy.

Before long, the double meaning of the puns in the strip took on political as well as social implications, and the vaudeville routines sometimes looked suspiciously like animals imitating people high in government. Just so we wouldn't miss the point, Kelly underscored his satirical intent with caricature: his animals had plastic features that seemed to change before our eyes until they resembled those at whom the satire was directed. And the species suggested something about Kelly's opinions of his targets. Russia's Nikita Khrushchev showed up one time as a pig; Fidel Castro as a goat. One consequence of this technique was that the verbal and the visual, the words and the pictures, were perfectly, inseparably, wedded—a supreme achievement in the art of the comic strip.

The first and undoubtedly the most powerful of Kelly's sequences in this satiric mode was his castigation of Senator Joseph McCarthy. McCarthy was then at the pinnacle of his fame and power as the nation's foremost crusader against Communists. His method—which was founded upon a basic disregard for the truth and included determining guilt by association and innuendo as well as deploying reckless accusation,

**123.** Scott Adams (Born 1957), **Dilbert** (about 1989-Present). October 13, 1996. Traces of graphite, pen and brown ink on illustration board, 8 × 18 in. (203 × 457 mm). Collection of Mark J. Cohen and Rose Marie McDaniel. Copyright © 1996. DILBERT reprinted by permission of United Feature Syndicate, Inc.

Adams' stark rendering of cubicle life in American offices is relentless in delivering a daily jibe at corporate America, its one-motive managers and its profit-driven objectives. The strip is startlingly true to life, its satire of documentary quality: Adams was the first syndicated cartoonist to give his e-mail address in his strip, and before long, enthusiastic readers regaled him with stories of the organizational nonsense they endured daily in their offices, supplying the cartoonist with a steady stream of material. Adams draws with a felt-tip pen, the ink of which fades to brown with age.

equivocation, and outright lying, not to mention character assassination and sheer intimidation—imparted a new word to the national lexicon: McCarthyism.

Kelly perceived that McCarthy was a charlatan, and proceeded in May 1953 to ridicule the senator and his methods in the strip. (Edward R. Murrow, the CBS correspondent revered for his courage and acumen, wouldn't attack McCarthy until almost a year later.) In later years, Kelly would provide alternative strips for newspapers to run in place of his sharpest satirical ones should his point of view be something the editors deemed offensive to their readers. But in 1953, Kelly showed not only artistic genius in his McCarthy sequence but great courage: given the popularity of McCarthy, Kelly risked cancellation by scores of newspapers whose readers were sympathetic to the senator's crusade.

Editorial cartoonists (led by Herblock) had skewered McCarthy regularly once the senator became well known. But syndicated comic strips in those days were still relatively free of political satire. Al Capp made fun of the rigid right, but no one named names. Kelly changed that. And as a cartoonist satirizing a national figure of McCarthy's power in a syndicated strip at the height of the senator's popularity, Kelly ran a greater risk than Murrow (who, in taking the public pulse before taking on McCarthy, had waited until McCarthy had almost hung himself before coming in to help with the noose). Newspaper editors are

(CONTINUED PAGE 154)

**124.** Brian Basset (Born 1957), **Adam @ Home** (June 24, 1984-Present). January 18, 1998. Pasteovers, pen and ink on illustration board, 9 1/2 × 13 in. (235 × 330 mm). Courtesy of the artist. ADAM @ HOME copyright © 1998 Brian Basset. Reprinted with permission of Universal Press Syndicate. All rights reserved.

Basset's strip focuses on a contemporary although not terribly widespread (yet) societal phenomenon—the hapless husband who stays at home to manage the household while the wife goes off to work every day. In recent months, Adam has established his own business at home, using a computer and the Internet. The combination of househusband and the electronic environment gives Basset ample opportunity to comment satirically on the impact of these innovations on individuals.

see page 150: **123.** Scott Adams, **Dilbert**

Mark and Rosie — Best Wishes, Scott Adams

Ray Billingsley

**125.** Ray Billingsley (Born 1957), **Curtis** (October 8, 1988 - Present). January 9, 1992. Blue pencil, pen and ink on illustration board, 4 1/2 × 14 3/4 in. (114 × 375 mm). Collection of the Cartoon Art Museum, San Francisco. Copyright © 1992. Reprinted with special permission of King Features Syndicate.

Set in an inner city, Curtis is about a feisty eleven-year-old African-American who lives with his younger brother and both parents. Wearing his hat backwards, Curtis is a typical kid having typical kid adventures at home and at school with his family and his teacher and classmates. Billingsley occasionally takes up racial issues but stresses that his strip is about relationships, not race.

notoriously timorous about the features in their papers. They listen to their readers with fear and trembling. Keeping readers happy keeps circulation steady; ditto editors' incomes. And it doesn't take many readers objecting to a syndicated feature to convince an editor that he risks losing circulation by provoking certain kinds of controversy. Syndicated features, aiming assiduously for universal acceptance—the greatest possible appeal—are consequently inclined to be studies in the most unobjectionable social fodder imaginable. And McCarthy was still a national hero to huge segments of the populace in the spring of 1953 when Kelly launched his attack. Substantial numbers of readers could have objected to Kelly's satire; and scores doubtless did. The cartoonist, scarcely Murrow's equal yet as a mover and shaker, was risking his very livelihood. To their everlasting credit, most newspaper editors stuck with him. But Kelly could not have known they would countenance his satire when he started; in fact, all the evidence of history would have convinced him that they would desert him in droves. The McCarthy sequence in *Pogo* is therefore a ringing testament to the cartoonist's courage.

To create a narrative metaphor for McCarthy's "commie hunt." Kelly turned to the swamp's Bird Watchers Club under the leadership of Deacon Mushrat [sic]. The Deacon is first joined by Mole MacCarony, who, despite his handicap (he can barely see), begins a program to purify the swamp of all germs. He then moves to rid the swamp of all "impurities," all "migratory birds"—that is, foreigners—but because he can't see well enough to identify his victims, it isn't long before everyone is under suspicion.

"What kind of an owl are you?" Mole asks Turtle.

"I ain't no owl," says Turtle. "I ain't even a bird."

"Were you ever a bird," asks Mole, imitating the inquisition techniques of McCarthyist investigatory bodies, "or are you thinking of becoming one?"

To assist in his work, Mole brings in a wild cat named Simple J. Malarkey, "a good wing shot and a keen eye." Malarkey gets himself elected president of the Bird Watchers Club by waving his shotgun under

**126.** Greg Evans (Born 1947), **Luann** (March 17, 1985-Present). May 22, 1985. Traces of blue pencil, pen and ink on illustration board, 4 × 12-1/2 in. (102 × 324 mm). Gift of the artist, The Ohio State University Cartoon Research Library. Copyright © 1985. LUANN reprinted by permission of United Feature Syndicate, Inc.

Evans has taken his strip far beyond the typical teenage dating themes that it might have embodied in another, earlier decade. In its first year—as evidenced here—the title character faces a typical teenager concern, and Evans treats the concern both sensibly and sensitively.

**127.** Greg Evans (Born 1947), **Luann** (March 17, 1985-Present). May 8, 1991. White gouache, pasteover, pen and ink on illustration board, 3 5/8 × 11 1/2 in. (92 × 292 mm). Gift of the artist, The Ohio State University Cartoon Research Library. Copyright © 1991. LUANN reprinted by permission of United Feature Syndicate, Inc.

When Evans did a series of strips in which his young heroine experiences her first menstrual period, he demonstrated beyond all question that a comic strip could deal with real life issues in a humorous yet informative and thoughtful manner.

Deacon's nose: "Betsey, here," says the leering cat, "got six or seven votes in her alone." The reign of terror and intimidation begins. Malarkey, in case you haven't guessed, looks remarkably like Joseph R. McCarthy, and the echo of McCarthy's technique is clear (FIGURE 113).

Faced with a number of swamp creatures who claim they aren't birds, Malarkey undertakes corrective action: "We'll jes' get some feathers an' some boilin' tar," says Malarkey, "an' with a little judicious application we can make the creature into any bird we chooses—all nice and neat."

At one satiric stroke, Kelly equated McCarthyism with an appropriately belittling analogue, tar-and-feathering—a primitive method of ostracizing that is universally held in low repute. In the delicious finale, Deacon, horrified by what he sees the Bird Watchers Club becoming, shoves Malarkey into the kettle of tar. Allegorical translation: those who seek to smear others are likely to be tarred with their own brush.

It was as neat a piece of satire as had ever been attempted on the comics pages or anywhere. And the success of it depended upon Kelly's plumbing the potential of his medium to its utmost. Word and picture worked in perfect concert: neither meant much when taken by itself, but when blended, the verbal and the visual achieved allegorical impact and a powerful satiric thrust. (And maybe the reason that Kelly got away unscathed is that newspaper editors in those innocent times did not recognize quickly enough that a masterful satire was taking place under their very noses—in the ever wholesome, perpetually inoffensive funnies!)

Kelly was to deploy these weapons again and again during the next twenty years. And all of the satiric action took place seemingly without the characters themselves being aware of it: the graphic portrayal of these denizens of the swamp as soft, plastic, and harmless joined the vaudevillian strain of the strip to proclaim the essential innocence of the characters, who went about their business, playing at being people, without being conscious of the larger, satiric implications of the acts (FIGURE 114). The result was a tour de force: humor at each of two levels—one vaudevillian, the other satirical. At times, the stories took on an allegorical cast; at times, the whimsical innocence of the creatures emerged in poignant commentary on the human condition.

*Pogo* opened to a greater extent than ever the possibilities for political and social satire in comic strips. Without *Pogo,* we'd surely have no *Doonesbury.* Garry Trudeau was able to name names in his strip because Kelly had broken the ground. Kelly's survival proved it could be done. And so in the next generation, Trudeau did it in *Doonesbury* (FIGURES 116-117). And even Cathy Guisewite did it in *Cathy* (briefly, terribly briefly). And although Berke Breathed's satire in *Bloom County* (FIGURE 121) was not as politically pointed as Trudeau's, Breathed was able to dare subjects and attitudes that, before Trudeau (and therefore before Kelly), would have been impossible.

With the greater license afforded cartoonists for political satire, the possibilities for social comment also opened up. And so we had Greg Evans confronting his heroine's first menstrual period in *Luann* (FIGURE 127), and Tom Batiuk pondering the question of the homeless in *Crankshaft* (FIGURE 129), and Ray

**128.** Greg Evans (Born 1947), **Luann** (March 17, 1985-Present). October 16, 1992. Traces of colored pencil, white gouache, pen and ink on illustration board, 3 5/8 × 11 5/8 in. (92 × 295 mm). Gift of the artist, The Ohio State University Cartoon Research Library. Copyright © 1992. LUANN reprinted by permission of United Feature Syndicate, Inc.

*Luann* doesn't focus all the time on sensitive teenage matters, but Evans periodically returns to subjects he knows will engage young readers, and he presents those subjects with a caring smile.

Billingsley portraying African-American family life in the inner city with his *Curtis* (FIGURE 125). These were not exactly satirical efforts, but they demonstrate that the range of subjects open to syndicated strip cartoonists has broadened. The champion at extending that range in recent years is clearly Lynn Johnston.

The characters in Johnston's comic strip about a family are all based upon her own family, her husband, her daughter, and her son. And herself. Although Elly, the mother in the fictional Patterson family, is named in memory of a childhood friend who died, the leading player in *For Better or For Worse* is, as Johnston says, "so very obviously, me." And Elly's trials and tribulations and triumphs are derived, one way or another, from Johnston's own experiences as a mother and wife.

When Johnston left the Vancouver (Canada) School of Art, she thought she was entering a career in animation. But she wound up producing slides for medical lectures at McMaster University Medical Center in Hamilton, Ontario. Later, pregnant with her first child and forced to await her obstetrician's attention in a prone position on his examining table, Johnston nagged him to put pictures on the ceiling so his patients would have something with which to occupy themselves while waiting, and he responded by asking her to furnish him with cartoons for the purpose. She did eighty, and at his urging they were published in 1974 as a booklet, *David, We're Pregnant!*

Johnston produced two more similar books, attracting the attention of an American syndicate, which invited her to submit a comic strip "about family life from a woman's point of view—something contemporary, a little controversial perhaps." The result (starting September 9, 1979) is a reality-based, warmly human strip that also generates the requisite controversy. In 1993, one of the son's teenage friends comes out

**129.** Tom Batiuk (Born 1947) and Chuck Ayers (Born 1947), **Crankshaft** (1987-Present). December 25, 1997. Pen and ink on paper, 2 3/4 × 8 3/4 in. (70 × 222 mm). Courtesy of Tom Batiuk. CRANKSHAFT copyright © 1997 Mediagraphics, Inc. Reprinted with permission of Universal Press Syndicate. All rights reserved.

Drawn by Ayers, *Crankshaft* explores the concerns of the elderly, the title character being well into that group. Here, on Christmas Day in 1997, Batiuk makes a poignant comment on homelessness, as Crankshaft, having been mugged in Central Park during a visit to New York, finds shelter in a crèche.

of the closet, announcing his homosexuality; two years later, the beloved family dog dies (FIGURES 132–135), and three years after that, so does Elly's mother. Such events are inevitable in a strip in which the characters grow up. But Johnston's strip is scarcely all controversy: to millions of readers, her characters are genuine people, humorously experiencing ups as well as downs in the ordinary business of daily living.

Other developments were also influential in contemporary newspaper strips. A whole new attitude toward subject matter was most strenuously pushed by the underground cartooning movement which began gathering momentum in the turbulent 1960s. Inspired by the irreverence of Harvey Kurtzman's epochal *Mad* comic book of the 1950s and its magazine-format descendants in subsequent years, college-age cartoonists began a nearly systematic assault on middle-class conventions. Drawing comic strips for counterculture, or "underground," newspapers in New York's East Village and in Berkeley, across the Bay from San Francisco, cartoonists like Bill Griffith and Gilbert Shelton produced comic strips deliberately designed to shock, visual-verbal assaults with sex and drugs as the weapons. These strips did not so much satirize social shibboleths as they flouted social mores. They slapped the puritanical middle-class in the face by showing pictures of people copulating and masturbating; these libidinous comics characters exposed hang-ups about sex by discarding every imaginable inhibition, thereby revealing the sexual neuroses of Western civilization. Comics that championed the drug culture of the sixties mimicked the tactic: in openly violating laws about drugs, the characters displayed their disdain for the society those laws were designed to protect.

**130.** Bill Griffith (Born 1944), **Zippy** (May 1986-Present). November 25, 1987. Traces of graphite, pen and ink on illustration board, 4 3/4 × 13 in. (121 × 330 mm). Collection of Mark J. Cohen and Rose Marie McDaniel. Copyright © 1987. Reprinted with special permission of King Features Syndicate.

Beginning in underground comic books in late 1970, Zippy the Pinhead graduated to national syndication with a unique brand of humor that Griffith deploys to expose our cultural preoccupation with American commerce. Wholly submerged in the artificial environment of advertising slogans, Zippy can't tell where the real world leaves off and the television world begins; and perhaps, Griffith seems to be saying, neither can we.

Underground cartoonists found their most fertile field in early 1968 when a young cartoonist named Robert Crumb produced his cartoons in comic book format, calling the booklet *Zap Comics* and selling copies of it out of a battered used baby carriage in the Haight Ashbury District of San Francisco, to which the flower children had begun flocking the previous summer. In retrospect, the first of the underground comic books (called "comix" to distinguish them from the mainstream product) was probably produced in late 1962 in Austin, Texas, by Gilbert Shelton. A post graduate hanger-on near the University of Texas where he'd edited the campus humor magazine, Shelton launched a series of short-lived guerrilla projects. Some of these featured cartoons drawn by his predecessor as editor of the *Texas Ranger,* Frank Stack, who was, by then, in graduate art school at the University of Wyoming in Laramie. Stack produced a series of strips that treated Jesus Christ irreverently (but gently) from the perspective of a person who has read the New Testament with an appreciation for the human predicament rather than an appetite for the divine message. (Jesus can't go swimming, for example; since he walks on water, it follows that he can't get submerged in it.) Vastly amused by these productions, Shelton photocopied pages of them, stapled them together, and distributed them among his friends: the first underground comic book!

Crumb's *Zap,* however, was a regular saddle-stitched magazine. And it was a cartooning venue much superior to the underground newspapers of the period. In the first place, the multi-page booklet afforded a cartoonist a much enlarged scope for his enterprises—and in a much more flexible format than the restrictive, single strip of panels to which newspapers confined cartoonists. In comic book format, cartoonists could treat subjects at greater length and, exploiting the page layout with varying sizes and configurations of panels, could achieve dramatic emphases undreamed of in the newspaper format. More significant, perhaps, was the economic benefit of the comic book: cartoonists were paid only a pittance for their

**131.** Frank Stack (Born 1937), **Dorman's Doggie** (about 1977-1979). January 1978. Pen and ink on paper, 9 1/4 × 14 in. (236 × 358 mm). Courtesy of the artist. Copyright © 1978 by Frank Stack.

One of the earliest underground cartoonists, Stack (signing his work Foolbert Sturgeon) created *Dorman's Doggie*, which was distributed to alternative newspapers. As in the example at hand, Ping (the existential poodle) is forever being "punished" for doing something quite reasonable or natural. He, like most of us, is surrounded and controlled by thoughtless, unreasonable beings who fail to understand him.

**132-136.** Lynn Johnston (Born 1947), **For Better or For Worse** (September 9, 1979-Present). April 14, 15, 18, 20, and 29, 1995. Traces of white gouache, applied half-tone film, pen and ink on paper, 3 ³/₈ × 10 ⁵/₈ in. (86 × 270) [each]. Lynn Johnston Collection, The Ohio State University Cartoon Research Library. © Lynn Johnston Productions, Inc./Dist. by United Feature Syndicate, Inc.

Johnston's warmly human strip chronicles the ordinary life adventures of a family, and while that life includes humorous events, it also includes tragedies—in the case at hand, the death of the family dog, who, before dying, performs the heroic act of saving the life of the youngest child in the family.

contributions to underground newspapers, but if they had the right printer for their comic book productions, they could keep a fair chunk of the revenue from the sales. And this financial fact spurred the growth of comix: cartoonists enjoyed not only editorial freedom but some measure of economic independence, too.

Shelton eventually drifted to California, and with a trio of other fugitives from Texas, he launched one of the underground's publishing empires, Rip-Off Press. Subsequently, Rip-Off established a syndicate for distributing underground comic strips to counter culture newspapers. Among the cartoonists who contributed work for this syndicate were Stack, who produced *Dorman's Doggie* (FIGURE 131), and Griffith, who created *Zippy* (FIGURE 130). Neither of these features was as offensive (in both senses) as some of the sex and drug material in comix, but both ventured into subjects not to be found in conventional comic strips. Dorman's doggie smelled and defecated like a dog; Zippy and his foil, Griffy (Griffith's self-caricature and alter ego), mocked the mainstream culture around them. In 1986, *Zippy* was picked up by a major feature syndicate and was soon appearing in mainstream papers across the land, but Griffith's unique brand of humor, brilliant though it is, scarcely spawned a following among cartoonists aspiring to create strips of their own. *Zippy* is, in fact, inimitable. Still, Griffith demonstrated that wholly unconventional, even eccentric, humor could find a home on the comics pages of the nation's newspapers. Gary Larson with his *Far Side* panel cartoon was providing a second vivid demonstration of the same sort of thing, and he had started his road show just a few years before Griffith.

Although the subject matter of comic strips had been steadily extended throughout the history of the artform, the form itself was severely limited in newspaper venues. Confined on weekdays to a lone horizontal strip of pictures, the daily comic strip had virtually nowhere to grow. In the Sunday funnies, however, cartoonists in the first decades of the century could experiment with the form itself, and they

produced a great variety of layouts, changing the shapes and sizes and arrangements of panels in order to achieve different special effects. But in the post–World War II years, even the Sunday comic strip format was hemmed in by economic considerations. Cartoonists were required to produce strips with "throw-away" panels, panels that editors could discard in order to publish the strips in a dimension smaller than the size of the cartoonist's initial conception. By dropping two panels, say, a given strip could be published as a quarter-page feature, enabling the editor to run three more Sunday strips on each page. The day of the full-page Sunday comic strip was long gone; and only a privileged few strips ran as half-page features (which included the two throw-away panels). Cartoonists met this challenge in various ways. Some produced elongated title-logo panels that could be discarded without damage to the day's joke or story. Some of the cartoonists simply produced two gag strips for Sunday—one in the opening two panels (that could be discarded), the other in the remaining panels of the strip.

Purely formal experimentation in the newspaper comic strip has been confined pretty much to the nature of the pictures in the prescribed strip form. Pat Brady and Bill Holbrook are particularly adventurous in this way. In *Rose Is Rose,* Brady plays with perspective, often creating visual puzzles in the opening panels of his strip, puzzles that the last panels "solve," the solution, the surprise of it, creating the day's gag

(FIGURE 98). In his *Fastrack* and *Safe Havens* strips, Holbrook frequently deploys images as an editorial cartoonist might—as symbols. In a given strip, a character may suddenly change shape or species to suggest an emotion that sheds comical light on the rest of the day's storyline (FIGURE 100). Jim Borgman and Jerry Scott in devising gags for their new strip, *Zits,* sometimes perform similar gymnastics with their visuals (FIGURE 108).

But these noble efforts in formal experimentation are the exception rather than the rule on the comics pages of newspapers. Most of the experimentation and the accompanying evolutions in the development of the cartooning art in the print medium have necessarily taken place in the more spacious comic book format. But that is another story for another time.[15]

And so here in the twilight of the twentieth century, we may safely ring down the curtain for the time being. If the past is any indication (and it often is), the comic strip will continue to evolve. Cartoonists will surely expand even more the range of subjects they can treat, and as the information superhighway takes us, willy-nilly, into cyberspace, the comic strip will doubtless adapt to this new way of disseminating information and entertainment. The next century in the history of the comic strip promises to be at least as innovative as the first century was. ●

## Discarding "Comics"

We use the term *comics* to describe things that are funny and things that aren't funny. The reasons for this anomaly are evident in the history of the medium. The newspaper supplement that Morrill Goddard produced in the fall of 1894 he presumably called a "comic weekly" because that's what he was imitating—the weekly humorous magazines like *Life, Judge, and Puck.* I have no etymological basis for presuming this (the *Oxford English Dictionary* is not very detailed on the matter), but my guess is that the term *comics* was associated in the popular mind both with the weekly magazines (as the OED has it and as I've indicated elsewhere herein) and with the humorous drawings in them. And then, once the *World* had shown the way to other papers, the term also came to embrace the colored comic Sunday supplements of daily newspapers. From this usage, it was but a short step to the use of *comics* to denominate the art form (comic strips) as distinct from the vehicle in which they appeared (the Sunday supplement itself). And once comic strips began to be reprinted in magazine form in the 1930s, the term was applied to those magazines, too—comic books became *comics.* Whether the evolution of the term followed these lines or not, the result is a confusing coinage. What, for instance, do we make of the assertion "Comics are art"?

Or is it, "Comics *is* art"?

Or are comics stand-up comedians?

The confusion inherent in the word *comics* has been apparent to those writing in the field for years. The word has a plural form but is singular in application. And in its singular form, *comic,* it can be an adjective for something humorous or another name for a comedian. In short, *comics* lacks the precision it ought to have for ordinary communication.

Let me submit an alternative. Let us derive a usage from the history of the medium. And let us start with the root of the word that is used for those who practice the art, *cartoonist.*

A *cartoonist* is one who draws *cartoons.* But *cartoon* is a relatively old word; *cartoonist* is wholly modern. Cartoon comes from the Italian *cartone,* meaning "card." Italian tapestry designers and fresco painters and the like drew their designs on sheets of cardboard at full scale before transferring those designs to the cloth or walls they were intended for. These designs were called by the name of the material upon which they were drawn—*cartones,* or *cartoons.* Later, the word *cartoon* was applied to any preliminary study for a final work.

But none of the artists who used cartoons in those days were called *cartoonists.* The word *cartoonist* is associated only with the medium known in modern times as *cartoon.*

The modern usage of *cartoon* began in London in the 1840s. It was first employed in the modern sense in reference to *Punch,* the London humor magazine. The Houses of Parliament had been all but destroyed in a fire in 1834. The building that took the place of the gutted relic was called the New Palace of Westminster and was built over the next decade. By the mid-1840s, it had been determined that the New Palace would contain various murals on patriotic themes, and a competitive exhibition was held to display the cartoons (in the ancient sense) submitted as candidates for these decorations. *Punch,* then only a couple years old, entered the competition on its own, publishing in its pages satirical drawings about government and calling them "Mr. Punch's cartoons." The first of these appeared in the weekly magazine dated July 15, 1843, and was greeted (we are told) with howls of joyous appreciation.

At first, *Punch* continued to call its humorous drawings "pencilings." Eventually, it applied the term *cartoon* to any full-page satirical drawing. But to the man in the street, any funny drawing in the magazine after the summer of 1843 was termed one of "Punch's cartoons," and by this route, the word came into use for any comic drawing. (See Herbert Johnson, "Why Cartoons—and How,"

*Saturday Evening Post,* July 14, 1928, p. 8, for a rehearsal of the *Punch* developments.) By the time Americans launched their imitations of *Punch* in the late 1800s, *cartoon* was well on its way to being established in the modern sense. And so was *cartoonist.*

As we've seen, the modern American newspaper cartoon started in the extravagant Sunday magazine supplements that Hearst and Pulitzer launched to attract buyers for their newspapers in the 1890s, frank imitations of the weekly humor magazines, *Life, Judge, Puck,* and a host of others—all of which traced their lineage back to *Punch* (and hence to its French inspiration, the Parisian journal, *Charivari).*

The persons who drew the humorous pictures in the supplements were sometimes called *comic artists* (because the pictures they drew were funny), but the term *cartoonist* was in use, too (and had been since at least the 1860s, if we are to judge from the *OED).* Thus, *cartoonist* is a word that has always referred specifically to the medium we now call *comics;* and *cartoonist* is the only word reserved exclusively for those who ply their skill in this medium. *Cartoonist* refers to nothing else. A *comic artist,* on the other hand, could refer to a comedian (who is a performing artist) or to an illustrator who draws humorous paintings (which are not necessarily cartoons).

Finally—to complete this historical review—comic books began when M. C. Gaines and a few like-minded entrepreneurs of the 1930s started reprinting newspaper cartoon strips in magazine format. With the success of the first of these ventures, the demand for material for such magazines grew so insistent that new stories had to be generated to fill the pages, and this original material drawn especially for the magazines continued to use the form of the cartoon strip to tell short stories. The magazines, then, might well be termed *cartoon story magazines* rather than *comic books* (particularly since many of them were not at all humorous and none of them were books).

By means of this etymological safari, we come at last to the terms I offer for the medium—terms exclusive to the medium and therefore incapable of the kind of semantic corruption that blurs meaning and distinction. I begin with *cartoonist,* the most exclusive of those terms.

A cartoonist may produce single-panel cartoons, animated cartoons, newspaper cartoon strips, or cartoon short stories (or cartoon story magazines). The word that embraces all these media is *cartoon.* It is the generic alternative to *comics.* And by adding the appropriate modifier, we can make *cartoon* accurately and precisely describe any of the genre in the medium.

I have no illusions that this campaign of mine will win any converts. And even if it does, I doubt that even legions of the converted would impinge much on the common parlance in which the term *comics* has come to apply to the medium. Language is like that. Its terms and usages are established by general practice, not by prescription. And English, perhaps more than any other language, is particularly open and receptive to this kind of evolution. Indeed, linguistically speaking, "English" is not a language at all: it is, rather, a sort of accumulation of usages and vocabularies, most derived from other languages. And this accumulation leaves us with *comics,* a term washed up on the beaches of the medium after weekly humor magazines had sunk into obscurity. We're doubtless stuck with its wobbly imprecision even if today we can think of better, more exact, terminology. Still, it's a nice notion to toy with.

## Notes

1. Coulton Waugh, *The Comics* (New York: Macmillan, 1947), p. 28. (hereafter Waugh)

2. Richard Olson, ed., *The R.F. Outcault Reader,* Vol. 3, No. 3; pp. 2-3.

3. Orison Sweet Marden, *Little Visits with Great Americans* (New York: Success Company, 1905), p. 355.

4. Ibid, pp. 355-56.

5. Moses Koenigsberg, *King News* (New York: F.A. Stokes, 1941), p. 450.

6. William E. Berchtold, "Men of the Comics," *New Outlook,* April 1935, p. 39.

7. Bud Fisher, "A Confession of a Cartoonist," *Saturday Evening Post,* July 28, 1928, p. 10. (hereafter Fisher)

8. John Wheeler, *I've Got News for You* (New York: Dutton, 1961), p. 145.

9. Fisher, p. 11.

10. Stephen Becker, *Comic Art in America* (New York: Simon & Schuster, 1959), p. 34.

11. Ron Goulart, *The Funnies: 100 Years of American Comic Strips* (Holbrook, Massachusetts: Adams, 1995), p. 25.

12. Quoted in Herb Galewitz, ed.,*Great Comics Syndicated by the Daily News-Chicago Tribune* (New York: Crown Publishers, 1972), p. ix.

13. Waugh, p. 176.

14. Robert C. Harvey, *Meanwhile: The Life and Art of Milton Caniff;* unpublished biography on file at the Cartoon Research Library, Ohio State University, Columbus, Ohio; p. 1283.

15. A story I undertake to tell in *The Art of the Comic Book* (University of Mississippi Press, 1996).

# A Brief Bibliography

## More History?

Anyone wishing to dig deeper into the subject is referred to the following (arranged by date of publication):

*Cartoon Cavalcade* by Thomas Craven. Simon and Schuster, 1943.

*The Comics* by Coulton Waugh. Macmillan, 1947 (reprinted by University Press of Mississippi, 1991.)

*Comic Art in America* by Stephen Becker. Simon and Schuster, 1959.

*The Comics: An Illustrated History of Comic Strip Art* by Jerry Robinson. Putnam's Sons, 1974.

*The Adventurous Decade* by Ron Goulart. Arlington House, 1975.

*The Encyclopedia of American Comics from 1897 to the Present* by Ron Goulart; Facts on File, 1990.

    A thoroughly competent and very readable general reference that includes comic books as well as comic strips.

*The Art of the Funnies* by Robert C. Harvey. University of Mississippi Press, 1994.

*The Art of the Comic Book* by Robert C. Harvey. University of Mississippi Press, 1996.

---

The centennial year of 1995 saw the publication of several books that were produced expressly
    to celebrate the occasion:

*The Yellow Kid*, assembled by Bill Blackbeard. Kitchen Sink Press.

*A Comic Strip Century*, (2 volumes) another Blackbeard production. Kitchen Sink Press.

*The Funnies: 100 Years of American Comic Strips* by Ron Goulart. Adams Publishing.

---

Four of the strips mentioned in this publication are being reprinted in their entirety:

*Pogo* (9 volumes so far, from the first strips in the 1948 *New York Star* through the summer of 1953),

*Little Orphan Annie* (to date, 5 volumes, 1931–1935), and *Prince Valiant* (so far, 32 volumes, 1937–1965)

Fantagraphics Books, 7563 Lake City Way N.E., Seattle, WA 98115

Ask for their catalogue by toll-free phone, 1-800-657-1100

*Li'l Abner* (26 volumes so far, 1934–1960)

Kitchen Sink Press, 76 Pleasant Street, Northampton, MA 01060

Phone free for a catalogue, 1-800-365-7465.

---

Several classic comic strips have been completely reprinted:

*Popeye* by E. C. Segar

*Little Nemo in Slumberland* by Winsor McCay

Fantagraphics [see address above]

*Terry and the Pirates* by Milton Caniff

*Wash Tubbs* by Roy Crane

*Tarzan* by Harold Foster and Burne Hogarth

NBM Publishers, 185 Madison Avenue, Suite 1504, New York, NY 10016

*detail*, **34.** Clifford McBride, **Napoleon**

# Comics as "Ding an Sich": A Note on Means and Media

RICHARD V. WEST

The German phrase *Ding an sich* translates as "the thing in itself." It was coined in the Age of Enlightenment by the German philosopher Immanuel Kant to signify the properties of an actual object, the raw data of its existence, as opposed to our perception and judgment of the object when we look at it. I have used the phrase to focus our attention on the rectangles of cardboard and paper with marks upon them, the "raw data" of the comic strip form. This investigation of "the thing in itself" is distinct from the issues of narrative and aesthetic content, personal style, and sociological portent that normally, and quite legitimately, govern the discussion of comic strips. Nor am I going to argue here whether or not comic strips are "fine art." Rather, my intent is closer to that of an archeologist: to draw (no pun intended) conclusions based on the evidence provided by the object itself, which in this case is the comic artist's "original" art work.

This raises the question of what we mean by the term "original" as applied to comic strip art. In many ways, the classification of the work of a comic strip artist defies traditional art-historical categories. For example, the comic strip "original" is not a sketch or study for a larger work in another medium. While a painter's or sculptor's preliminary studies and studies often provide valuable insights about an artist's intent and approach, they are not considered the artist's final word on the subject. By this definition, the comic strip "original" is not a preliminary sketch, but a finished work. Yet, it is definitely not the final form of the strip. Does that mean that the comic strip in its printed newspaper form is the "original?" Well, it certainly is the "end product" that was intended (more or less) by the artist, but it is not an "original" in the sense of a unique or limited object. The critical difference between "original" and "end product" is important to our understanding of the special situation of the comic strip artist and is due, in large part, to the nature of the newspaper business. There are many steps between the unique set of drawn images created by the comic strip artist and the way those images appear in the daily newspaper, steps that are not necessarily under the artist's control and are often governed by economic and editorial imperatives.

If the purpose of the comic strip "original" is to provide the basis for multiple copies, does that make it a form of printmaking? Here, too, there are crucial differences of technique and intent. In order to produce a print (sometimes called a "multiple original"), an artist engraves a metal plate, carves on a wood block, or draws on a lithographic stone to create a matrix from which a number of images are printed. Typically, "multiple originals" are printed by the artist who created the matrix or under his or her close supervision, and the limited number of prints so produced are individually signed and numbered to create an "edition." Since the matrix is usually considered a means to an end, it is generally destroyed, disfigured, or reused for other images after the edition is complete. This also assures the limited nature of the fine art print edition. The methods and aims of producing the comics are quite different from printmaking. Normally, the comic artist is only required to produce the drawing; the preparation and printing of his images are tasks handled by others. Also the goal of comic production is the widest dispersal through unlimited copies. There is nothing precious or rarified about the business.

There are some historical examples of "multiple originals" that are closer to the aims and methods of producing comic strips. For example, Honoré Daumier, the great nineteenth-century artist who satirized the mores and politics of France in the 1830s and 1840s, used the lithographic process to make numerous copies of his caricatures for publications such as *La Charivari* and *La Caricature*. Unlike twentieth-century comic artists, however, Daumier usually drew directly on the lithographic stone, the matrix, which was reground and used to create a fresh image after a sufficient number of images were pulled from it. The only "originals" are the images that exist on the pages of Parisian periodicals or the special editions that were made of certain caricatures.

In the case of comics, the original drawing can't be considered the "matrix" for the printed version. The true matrix is the printing plate produced by photo-mechanical means from the artist's drawing. Like many other matrices, the printing plate is normally discarded or recycled after it has served its purpose. Fortunately for us, the inked drawing is not destroyed (at least not intentionally) in the process of making the plate, and remains as a sort of "proto-matrix" from which, presumably, a new matrix could be made.

Despite the conclusion that there may be no comic strip "original" in the literal sense of the word, the fact remains that the drawn object, the *Ding an sich,* is closest to the artist and may reveal aspects of the craft and insights into the creative process that are diluted and lost in the reproductive process. For all intents and purposes the inked drawing *is* the original, and will be considered as such in this discussion.

These originals are almost always rectangles of commercially produced card stock or stiff paper upon which the artist has produced his or her images. In traditional terminology, the cardboard is the "support" and the means used to create the images is called the "medium." The most commonly used medium during the first century of comic strips has been (and remains) black ink applied with a pen or brush. Yet a close look at the originals reveals a variety of other media. Frequently there are traces of graphite left from the original pencil sketches underlying the inked images. On many originals, blue pencil is used to make the preliminary sketches, to produce the ruled lines for lettering, and to record notes and annotations to printer about textures and colors. Since it isn't detected by the photo-mechanical process that translates the original drawing into its final newspaper form, blue pencil lines are normally not erased, thus providing a fascinating insight into a comic strip artist's creative process (FIGURE 114). In order to enliven the stringent black and white norm of the strips, some artists apply various textured films (FIGURE 118) or use specially prepared boards that produce texture by chemical action (FIGURE 52).

Artists sometimes change their minds (or even make mistakes): hence the frequent appearances of white overpaint, scratched out sections, or pasted over and redrawn areas (FIGURE 49). Comic strip artists also resort to pasteovers to drop in frequently used title panels (FIGURES 88, 121) or to insert an image acquired from another source, such as a tracing based on a photograph (Figure 83). In all cases, artists count on the forgiving process of translation from original to printed form to hide these various maneuvers. Probably the biggest surprise for many newspaper readers is the fact that the originals intended for the Sunday strips are also created in black and white. Although the artist indicates how the color and textures are to be applied through a color key (FIGURES 6, 12) or color-coded notations on the original (FIGURE 34), the ultimate result is in the hands of the engravers and printers. Carefully colored originals do exist, however, usually the result of a special presentation or gift on the part of the artist (FIGURES 23, 53, 78).

For a reader accustomed to comic strips as they are reproduced in contemporary newspapers, the size of the originals is a revelation. This is particularly marked in the originals of earlier strips, which were created at a time when newspapers were larger in format and greater space was allotted for the funnies. In the first decade or so of this century, an original for a Sunday feature could measure almost thirty inches in height (FIGURE 8), while a daily is almost the same in width (FIGURE 10). A few artists were able to maintain this size into the middle of the century (FIGURES 55-56). These generous dimensions allowed scope for grandeur as well as subtlety in execution. Even in the case of contemporary strips, shrunken as they are by economic and editorial edicts, the original drawings are usually thirty to fifty percent larger than the reproduced image (FIGURES 101, 123).

The present condition of many comic strip originals is often alarming, but not surprising given the process of creation. Until very recently, the original was considered a means to an end, so many artists and editors gave no thought to the preservation of these objects. Once reproduced, the original lost its purpose. It is miraculous that so many examples of earlier strips survived at all; those that have often bear witness to hard knocks, spilled coffee, and other indignities. Often, larger strips were cut up to make mailing them to the engravers easier (FIGURE 111), while others were cut up into separate panels as gifts or donations (FIGURE 67).

The most disturbing aspect of the condition of comic strip originals is what art conservators call "inherent vice," that is, the deterioration of the object due to inferior materials. Since the original had no intrinsic value except as the basis for photo reproduction, artists tended to use the cheapest materials they could find. The so-called "illustration board" used by many artists is a mass-produced item made from highly acidic pulp paper. As it ages, it turns brown and self-destructs rapidly, becoming brittle and weak. This condition accelerates with exposure to direct sunlight or moisture and is aggravated by applications of masking tape, rubber cement, or half-tone films, which eventually peel off leaving stains and residues. It should be noted that some contemporary cartoon artists are now using better quality bristol board (a pressed, coated, stiff card stock) or high-quality drawing papers such as Strathmore.

The dense black ink used by many comic strip creators, often called "India ink," is quite stable, but the same cannot be said for other inks. "Permanent" marker pen inks are anything but, and eventually fade to shadows. Watercolors often contain fugitive pigments that turn or fade over time, especially if exposed to strong light. Ironically, Renaissance and Baroque sketches, drawn on the pure rag papers of the period, will probably survive longer than many of the comic strip originals created within the last hundred years unless great care is exercised in the future. Fortunately, there are now archives, research libraries, museums, and serious private collections where the inevitable decay of the comic strip original is reduced to the minimum through proper care and treatment. For this, we should be grateful. Although the comic strip image can be reproduced ad infinitum in every form from printed to digital, the comic creator's original drawing, often visually far richer than the "end product" can ever be, is a vital link in our understanding and appreciation of this lively art form. ●

# Index

Illustrations are indicated with **bold** typeface.
Caption information is indicated with c, eg. 84c.
Characters are alphabetized by their first name.